LACE
from the Attic

A VICTORIAN NOTEBOOK OF KNITTED LACE PATTERNS

NANCIE WISEMAN

INTERWEAVE PRESS

Cover design, Susan Wassinger, Signorella Graphic Arts
Photography, Joe Coca
Technical Editing, Dorothy T. Ratigan

Interweave Press, Inc.
201 East Fourth Street
Loveland, Colorado 80537–5655
USA

Printed in the United States of America by United Graphics

Library of Congress Cataloging-in-Publication Data

Wiseman, Nancie, 1950–
    Lace from the attic: a Victorian notebook of knitted lace
patterns/by Nancie Wiseman.
      p. cm.
    Includes index.
    ISBN 1–883010–40–3 (paperbound)
    1. knitted lace—Patterns.   I. Title.
TT805.k54W57   1998
746.2'26041—dc21   98–4351
                                          CIP

First Printing:IWP—7.5M:698:UG

Contents

ACKNOWLEDGMENTS

First and foremost I thank Miss Blanche Beau for taking the time to write and knit all these wonderful lace patterns. I'm sure she never knew what a true work of art she was producing and how much we would appreciate it so many years later. Thanks to Madeline Eid for giving me the book, and to her sister Ann Stomsvik; you were both a huge help and a wonderful source of information. Thanks also to Joe and Julie Wolfenden for opening their home and allowing me to see where Miss Blanche Beau lived and died.

Thanks to my husband, William R. Attwater, who tolerated lace all over the house and my constant knitting, even on vacation. He often wondered aloud if he would get lace on his underwear some day. He never failed to tell me something was "pretty" when I asked, and always made a joke about "What are we going to do with that?" Your constant love and support are always with me.

My three dogs, Christina, Polly, and Bowser sat by me for endless hours as I knitted, wrote, and figured out abbreviations and patterns. They were always ready to go for a walk when I needed to take a break.

Thanks to my mother Thayes M. Wiseman, who passed away before the work on this book began, for giving me the strength and talent to create. Thank you for teaching me to knit and crochet as a child. Your strong will, strength, and persistence remain with me always.

Thanks to my customers and employees who kept my shop running while I wrote this book. Marlene Fong shouldered more responsibility than she bargained for when she first came to work—thank you for being my friend. Thanks to all of you for remaining loyal and tolerating my one-track mind.

Thanks to my dear friends Laura Bryant of Prism Yarns, Carol Wigginton, founder of The Knitting Guild of America, and Susan Hamilton, editor of *Cast On*—your proofreading and suggestions were a huge help. Your support and phone calls were always welcome and always came when I needed them most. Carol's simple comment, "I'm so proud of you," means more than she will ever know. I will always be grateful to you all.

Kaethe Kliot, owner of Lacis in Berkeley, California, offered help and encouragement as well as expertise in all aspects of lace making.

Thanks to the Sacramento Room of the Sacramento Public Library for their interest in the original notebook and its history and for help in the historical research.

And, of course, thanks to everyone at Interweave Press, especially my editor Judith Durant, for constant help and support in producing this book, a true labor of love.

INTRODUCTION

It will always be one of my fondest keepsakes—an aged leather notebook filled with lace samples knitted long ago, left in an attic, and eventually entrusted to my care. The samples and their directions became more than the basis for this book; they led me on a path of creative challenge, historical research, and personal discovery. They led me to a friend whom I have never met, but nonetheless feel I know very well. The more I learned about the original notebook and its owner, the more certain I was that it was meant to be mine. The coincidences and similarities between my life and the author's were so compelling that I felt no one could love this treasure more than I.

I have owned Nancie Knits in Sacramento, California, for about eleven years now. I have many fond memories of customers and their stories as well as their knitting and crochet projects. But the greatest and fondest is of the day Madeline Eid walked into my store with the notebook. With just a few brief words and a small explanation of its background, she handed me the fragile book and said, "I'll never be able to do anything with this, but I thought you could." At the time, I was not aware of just how much pleasure the book would ultimately bring me.

I carefully looked through it. I marveled at the small pieces of lace knitting that were attached to and tumbling out from every page. I then began to examine the individual pages and the handwritten directions for each of the samples, a beautiful Victorian scroll done in fountain pen. It's the type of handwriting I've always wished I had. I also noticed that the directions were not written in any format I had ever seen before. The abbreviations were completely different, and not always consistent. Interpreting these patterns would be a challenge.

I put the book away in as safe a place as I could find in the storeroom of my shop, but it was never very far from my mind. On slow days I would putter around, see the book out of the corner of my eye, and just have to sit down with a cup of tea and look at it again. As I studied the samples and directions, some of the abbreviations began to make sense. I had to use a magnifying glass to examine the small pieces because many weren't much larger than a postage stamp. I would occasionally try to figure out one or two of the directions, and then other obligations would take over and I would have to put the book away.

I've known from the start that this notebook is something to be shared with anyone who knits or enjoys history, that it is simply too wonderful to keep to myself. But what if something happened to it before the patterns were interpreted? It was almost lost to the trash pile once; I didn't want that to happen again.

The adventure finally went into full swing in the spring of 1996 when I decided to spend more time knitting and interpreting the laces. I always knew that the notebook would make a wonderful story, but when I learned about the life of the original owner, I knew not only that the book was meant to be mine, but also mine to share.

The more I worked on the patterns and began to "think" like the author, the more obsessed I became with getting all the laces knitted and into a book. Thankfully, the wonderful people at Interweave Press agreed with me, and the historical search, as well as the knitting and writing, began in earnest.

HOW IT ALL BEGAN

The 100-year-old notebook that is the basis of this book was found in the attic of the house where a Miss Blanche Beau had lived. My friend Madeline Eid's brother, Lynn C. Peyton, had inherited the large Victorian home at 725 21st Street in downtown Sacramento, California, from Miss Beau in 1966. Sixteen years later, when age and declining health led him to sell the home, he discovered many of Blanche's possessions still in the attic and closets. The notebook of lace and knitting instructions was rescued from the trash pile and given to Madeline, who then gave it to me.

I immediately felt a strong kinship with Blanche Beau—after all, she loved knitting as much as I do—and I first spoke about her with Madeline and her sister Ann. They remembered visiting their brother at Blanche's house during the early 1960s. Blanche was quite elderly by this time and would usually stay up in her room, resting. They remembered that she wore a wig but recalled little else about her appearance. One of their most vivid memories was of Blanche's standard poodle, Harlan. He usually stayed with her while she rested. He was, to their recollection, Blanche's pride and joy.

Ann had saved some of Blanche's things—charming place-card holders that Blanche had probably made, invitations to weddings dating to the 1890s, and some March 1937 information from the Sacramento Garden Club on how to grow camellias. Blanche loved camellias, the city flower of Sacramento, and they were planted all around her home.

Among Blanche's things was a poignant letter from Mrs. Nellie M. Warren of Plymouth, California, dated July 23, 1942. Blanche would have been sixty-six years old at the time. A portion of the letter reads as follows:

Dear Miss Blanche Beau,

In answer to your inquiry I will say your mother was buried on a hill north of the house where they lived. I was there once with some friends. The only time I ever saw your mother I was only a young girl then and you were a baby perhaps nearly a year old. Not so very long after that your mother died and all the neighbors attended her funeral. . . .

I don't know anything about your grandparents and all the old-timers are gone who could have told you all about them.

Mrs. Warren

I don't know if Blanche went to find her mother's grave, but I think it is very sad that in her later years she still wanted to find out where her mother had been buried.

Blanche's parents had immigrated from France and settled in Plymouth, a small town in the foothills east of Sacramento, during the gold rush of the 1850s. Mrs. Warren's letter told me that Blanche's mother had died when Blanche was about a year old. I learned that after her mother passed away, Blanche was brought from Plymouth to Sacramento to be raised with her cousin Louise by her aunt and uncle, Mr. and Mrs. Leon Pesron.

I eventually found Blanche's death certificate and her obituary, as well as some information on the house where the notebook was found. Blanche was born on June 17, 1875, and she passed away on November 29, 1966. According to the City Directories located at the Sacramento Library, from 1895 to 1899 Blanche worked as a bookkeeper for a local bakery on 3rd Street in downtown Sacramento. In 1899, she went to work for the State Printing Office at the state capitol. I was unable to find out how long she worked there, or if she ever worked anywhere else in the city.

I got the idea that if I could get into the house where the notebook came from I could learn more about where and how Blanche lived. I don't know exactly what I expected to find, but I knew I had to try. I wrote a "Dear Resident" letter to the current owners.

Joe Wolfenden had been collecting information on his wonderful old home, and he phoned me as soon as he got my letter. He was excited to find someone else who was researching his home and its former occupants. We decided to meet at the house to share information and photographs.

My visit was on a sunny day in May. Joe and his wife Julie Wolfenden are wonderful, friendly people who have worked very hard to bring the house back to its original splendor. The grand porch where people spent summer evenings catching the cool breeze off the river, the large banisters, and the huge camellia bush in the front yard were simply breathtaking. My walk through the foyer with a library on the left and stately living and dining rooms on the right was a walk back in time. The house has large rooms with grand wooden floors and paneling that, thanks to Joe and Julie, have been restored to their original dark wood.

Blanche Beau

We sat at the large dining table and pored through our information. Joe had wonderful pictures that had been left in the home. We talked about the people in the photographs as though we had known them all our lives. We found one photograph of Miss Blanche Beau taken in about 1902. She would have been about twenty-seven years old.

We turned our attention to the house. Although it was built by her cousin Louise, Blanche is listed as owner. Louise was a widow, and she and Blanche probably worked together to get the ten-room, two-story house built. Once it was finished, Louise, her daughters Emma and Berta, her mother, and Blanche moved in about 1912. Following Louise's death in 1934, Blanche started renting out rooms. Two gentlemen, Lynn C. Peyton and Robert C. Taylor, boarded at the home for many years, and eventually cared for Blanche until her death.

When Blanche passed away, her estate included the house and many properties within the city of Sacramento; Mr. Peyton and Mr. Taylor inherited all the properties, as well as many personal items.

My tour of the house revealed history and charm everywhere. I was lead into the room where Blanche had passed away, a room at the front of the house with a lovely view of the street below. The environment of stately trees and Victorian houses must have been a comforting one to grow old in. The street is much busier now, and the view very different than in Blanche's time, but it remains lovely.

This May afternoon took me on a trip back to a time when life was quieter and grander, to the home of an elegant and charming woman who spent her later days with her collections of lace and her beloved poodle. As it turned out, I'd learned all I would ever know about Miss Blanche Beau, but now I could picture her in her living room or on the grand porch, working on her projects, collecting lace in her notebook.

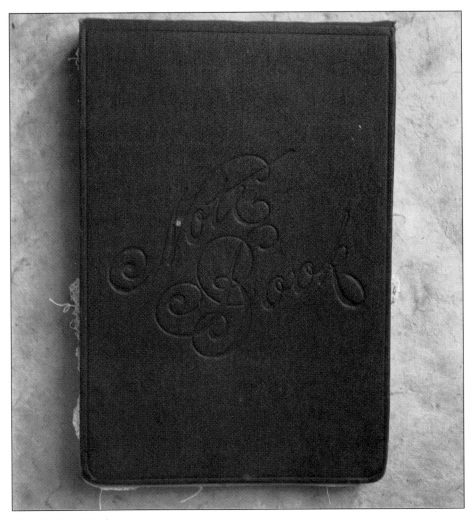

Blanche's notebook

Solving the Pattern Mystery

I felt much like an archeologist interpreting hieroglyphics as I sat with the mysterious abbreviations used in Blanche's notebook. Some were easy to figure out, others more difficult. But with lots of patience and knitting, I solved them all and even corrected some of Blanche's mistakes. This is by far the most interesting knitting I've ever done.

Some of the abbreviations she used were quite obvious; "O" for yarn over was probably the easiest one to figure out. Another obvious abbreviation was "N" for knit two together, which always seemed to be associated with "O". Generally, lace knitting involves a decrease for every increase. In this case the "O" was for an increase and the "N" for a decrease.

"N" is actually an abbreviation for "narrow", although the meaning is the same as "decrease". In one pattern, Blanche used the abbreviation "N3tog", probably to mean "narrow three together" or "knit three together" as we know it today.

I needed counting and math to figure out many abbreviations. Since I always knew how many stitches the patterns started with, I could count through the first row and try to make the number of stitches I had fit the number of stitches the pattern told me to use. Another way that counting helped is that I could knit a partial row and then count backwards from the written direction to see if it would work on the number of stitches that remained. This was really helpful on patterns with more than twenty stitches.

One abbreviation that gave me some trouble was "OSN". I knew the "O" meant yarn over, the "S" probably meant slip one stitch, and the "N" I'd already figured for knit two together. But this interpretation only worked for one row—the subsequent row came out with one too many stitches. After thinking about it, I realized one would seldom, if ever, in lace knitting, slip one stitch in the middle of a row without passing that stitch over another stitch. So in working the abbreviation "OSN" as yarn over, slip one, knit two together, and pass the slipped stitch over, the pattern worked.

Another poser was "S and B". Again, counting helped, and I determined that it had to be a decrease: slip one, knit one, pass the slipped stitch over. Blanche had used "B" to mean "bind off" in some of her directions, so I determined that here she must mean to bind off a stitch in the middle of a row, which is what slip one, knit one, pass the slipped stitch over does. So to Blanche, "S and B" meant slip and bind off.

Later in the book she changed her abbreviations, and some were more like those we see today. Other directions combine Blanche's earlier abbreviations with modern ones. There were occasional pencil notations such as "wrong" or "pretty", and in places she wrote over a direction to change it. While working one of the patterns labeled "wrong", I proceeded cautiously. The directions turned out to be just fine, so I realized that Blanche made knitting errors like the rest of us.

In a few patterns it wasn't clear what part of a direction to repeat; there weren't the parentheses or asterisks we use today. Blanche's spacing sometimes helped determine how much of a direction to repeat, as did the small dashes she used between abbreviations. But for the most part, the only way to figure out a repeat was by charting and counting.

One helpful thing that Blanche did was put a period at the end of each row, as though it was a sentence. Sometimes lines overlapped in her handwritten directions, so I wouldn't have been sure where a row ended if it weren't for the period.

Keep in mind that not only were the abbreviations different, they were written in a beautiful Victorian scroll with a fountain pen. Toward the back of the book the handwriting changes slightly, becoming heavier and bigger, apparently as Blanche aged.

Part of one page had been torn out of the book. This worried me at first, but the row numbers continued as they should on the next page. Perhaps Blanche had made a mistake and decided to just tear off half the page rather than cross it out.

It appears that someone other than Blanche made notes in the back of the book. The book had been flipped over and the back was used as though it was the beginning. There are quite a few pages of ramblings in a different handwriting from Blanche's. Fortunately, nothing was done to destroy the laces or directions.

It was very helpful to have Blanche's knitted samples sewn to the page with the directions. Some are as small as a postage stamp and I had to use a magnifying glass to see the intricate pattern details.

Mikado Lace
Updated Pattern

CO 22 sts.

Set-up row: Knit.

Row 1: K2, yo twice, k2tog, k10, [yo twice, k2tog] 3 times, k2—26 sts.

Row 2: K4, [p1, k2] 2 times, p1, k12, p1, k2.

Rows 3, 4, 7, 11, and 15: Knit.

Row 5: K2, [yo twice, k2tog] 2 times, k12, [yo twice, k2tog] 3 times, k2—31 sts.

Row 6: K4, p1, [k2, p1] 2 times, k14, [p1, k2] 2 times.

Rows 8 and 12: K2, [k2tog, k1] 8 times, k2tog, k3—22 sts.

Row 9: K2, [yo twice, k2tog] 9 times, k2—31 sts.

Rows 10 and 14: K4, p1, [k2, p1] 8 times, k2.

Row 13: K2, [yo twice, k2tog] 9 times, k2—31 sts.

Row 16: BO 9, k21—22 sts.

Repeat Rows 1–16 for desired length. BO on Row 16.

Mikado Lace

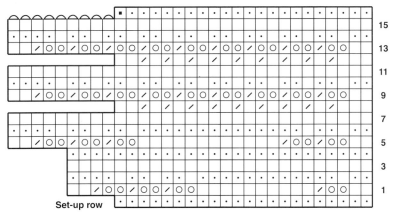

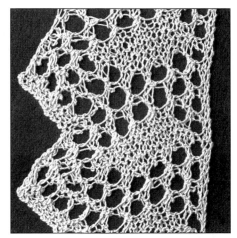

Other directions had no sample attached, and some loose samples had been randomly stuck in the book.

Blanche copied some patterns from magazines and may have gotten others from friends. "The Delineator Leaf Lace" and "Ladies' Home Journal Edging" most certainly came from magazines. *The Delineator* was a Victorian-era ladies magazine, and *Ladies' Home Journal* probably predated the magazine we see on the newsstand today. Laces that may have come from friends are "Mrs. Belli's Diamond Lace" and "Mable Casis's Lace". Seven laces are simply called "Knitted Lace". Some are wide, some are narrow. I have called them "Knitted Lace #1", "Knitted Lace #2", etc. for clarity.

Because not all the patterns were original, Blanche probably made some errors in transcription. But certain abbreviations most likely were her own; I have not found them anywhere else. After knitting all the laces, I discovered that some were duplicates under different names. This fact supports my theory that Blanche worked on the notebook for many years and didn't realize that she was knitting the same lace twice.

In any lace direction, the abbreviations begin to make sense after you work with them for a short time. In fact, once I got used to Blanche's abbreviations I found them much easier than the ones we use today, and they take up considerably less space. For example, "N" for knit two together, is much quicker to write than "k2tog".

Blanche's directions eventually became so easy for me to follow that it was almost as if I had been programmed to knit the laces, as though my brain was "hardwired" for the patterns and abbreviations. I say this because, for some laces, I can't really tell you how I figured them out. They just came naturally. Sounds weird, I know, but I honestly feel that somewhere in my "knitter's brain" the seeds of these lace patterns had already been planted.

TOOLS AND TECHNIQUES

THREAD AND YARN

A wide variety of yarns and threads can be used for lace knitting. Commonly known as crochet cotton, these threads include Coats Patons Opera, Anchor, and DMC Cebelia, Baroque, Perle Cottons, and Cordonnet, and they come in many sizes and colors. Trims and borders are traditionally done in cotton, linen, or silk. If you are new to lace knitting, I recommend that you do your first project in a fingering or sport-weight wool, which is more forgiving and easier to work with than cotton. Using large needles for this project can eliminate frustration and allow you to see just how simple lace knitting is.

The samples shown at right, from top to bottom, were knitted with:

Thread size	Needle size
5	3
10	2
20	1
30	0
40	00
50	000
60	0000
70	00000
80	000000

Crochet and knitting cottons come in a variety of sizes that range from 5, which has the largest diameter, to 100, which is similar to sewing thread. As you can see in the samples, one pattern can yield many different effects with changes of thread and needle size. A large pattern with many stitches can be knitted on fine needles to produce a narrow border. Conversely, a narrow pattern can be knitted with large

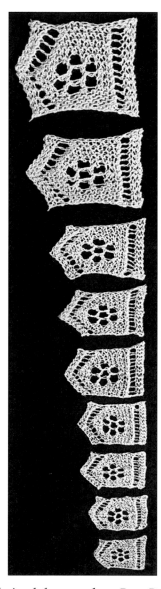

I knitted the same lace, Rose Point Lace, with nine different threads on nine different-sized needles.

thread and needles to produce a wide border. Lace patterns can be knitted in most weights of yarn to yield pleasing borders for sweaters, hats, scarves, or afghans.

Compared to the amount of yarn needed for a sweater, the amount of thread needed for most lace borders in this book is amazingly small. Most crochet and knitting thread is sold in 50-gram balls, so the yardage will vary depending on the thread size; the thicker the thread, the less the yardage. One ball of thread will produce enough border for many projects. The handkerchief border shown on page 76 was done with size 40 thread on 0000 needles and took less than one ball. The border around the tablecloth shown on page 73 was knitted in size 10 Coats Patons Opera on size 3 needles and took three and one-half balls. If you plan to knit a very long border, see how much of the border one ball of your chosen type of yarn will knit and then plan from that the total number of balls of the same dye lot to buy for the whole project.

NEEDLES

Sizes of knitting needles vary greatly to complement the different sizes of thread. And contrary to popular belief, lace does not *have* to be knitted on tiny needles. In fact, larger needles can produce lacier knitting. Needles range in size from the tiniest 00000000, also referred to as 8-0 or 8-aught, up to the traditional sizes used for garment and afghan knitting. Most borders dealt with here are small enough to be worked with a pair of double-pointed needles. In fact, many of the smallest needles are available only as double-pointed needles, which are designed for knitting in the round. All needles smaller than size 0 are metal (other materials aren't strong enough for such small diameters); larger needles are available in metal, wood, and plastic. You may find wooden needles easier to work with than metal—they're not so slippery and the blunt points will not poke holes in your fingers.

> **Tip**
> Metric measures on U.S. needles vary depending on manufacturer. If you use American needles, be sure to use the same brand throughout a project for consistent results.

MARKERS

You can use markers to keep track of pattern repeats or changes in stitch patterns, especially when you're working large doilies or shawls. However, they may simply get in the way when you're working lace borders, which tend to have fewer stitches. Most commercially-available markers are so thick compared to fine lace needles that they may affect the gauge in nearby stitches, especially when you use cotton thread (which has no memory). For such projects, make your own markers from small loops of colored thread.

There are times when you need to mark stitches that have already been knit, rather than those on the needles. For these use split-ring markers or, better yet, knitter's safety pins—stainless steel or brass safety pins that have no coils that can get tangled in the thread.

TAPESTRY AND SEWING NEEDLES

Use a tapestry needle to graft stitches together. Tapestry needles come in various sizes, but all have blunt tips and relatively large eyes. The size to use depends on your project; size 18 to 20 needles are appropriate for size 5 threads. Use needles up to size 28 for finer threads or for sewing borders directly to fabric. Because sewing needles have sharp points that can split threads, take care to place the needle *between* the threads, not through them, when grafting or sewing to fabric.

Row Counters

All lace patterns require meticulous row counting. To help, manufacturers provide many styles and sizes of row counters that fit on knitting needles or sit on a table. (Note that counters that fit on needles are generally too large for fine lace knitting, will fall off double-pointed needles, and can add awkward weight to small needles.) You can also use pencil and paper. Choose whichever method is easiest for you and use it throughout the project. The biggest challenge to any of these methods is remembering to do it.

Because many lace patterns have garter-stitch backgrounds, right- and wrong-side rows can look similar. The first row of a lace pattern is usually a right-side row. Note whether the cast-on tail is on the left or right of the knitting when you begin this row. The tail will be on the same side for all following right-side rows. If all right- or all wrong-side rows begin the same way, you can use this fact as a check that you are on the row you think you are.

Point Protectors

You will find that small needles can be very sharp and may poke through your knitting bag. Use point protectors on the needle tips to guard against this danger and to prevent stitches from falling off. Use two-holed point protectors for double-pointed needles, placing the tips of two needles in each protector. This will protect the tips from breaking or bending and will help prevent lost needles.

Knitting Techniques

Casting On (CO)

The cast-on for lace knitting should be firm but not tight. To prevent stitches that are too tight, work the cast-on over two needles and then remove one before you begin knitting.

The Long-Tail or Slingshot method of casting on is preferred for lace knitting. This method is also known as Continental.

Long-Tail Cast-On Use two needles together as one. Leaving a tail long enough for the desired number of stitches, make a slip knot and place it on the needles. Place the thumb and index finger of your left hand between the two threads. Secure the long ends with your other three fingers. Twist your wrist up so that your palm faces upward, and spread your thumb and index finger apart to make a V of the yarn. You now have four strands of yarn, 1, 2, 3, and 4 (Figure 1; note that a single needle is shown).

Place the needle under strand 1, from front to back. Place the needle over the top of strand 3 (Figure 2) and bring the needle down through the loop around your thumb (Figure 3). Drop the loop off your thumb and, placing your thumb back in the V configuration, tighten up the resulting stitch on the needle.

When the required number of stitches have been cast on, remove the extra needle and stretch the stitches evenly across the remaining needle. You should see a small gap between each stitch.

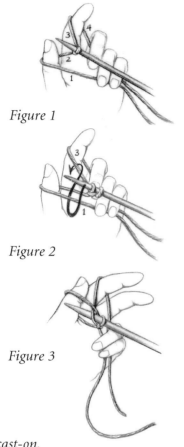

Figure 1

Figure 2

Figure 3

Long-tail cast-on.

Provisional Cast-On If you want to graft the beginning edge to the ending edge, use a cast-on that can be removed once the knitting is completed, leaving live stitches that can be grafted to other live stitches and making the knitting appear continuous and seamless.

To begin, knot the working yarn to a length of contrasting waste yarn. Use your right thumb to hold the knot against a knitting needle in your right hand.

Hold the yarns in your left hand with the working yarn over your index finger and the waste yarn over your thumb. Work as for the long-tail method, inserting the right needle up into the waste yarn on your thumb, around the working yarn on your index finger, and down through the waste-yarn loop on your thumb. Remove your thumb from the loop and pull the needle gently to adjust the tension. Repeat until you have the desired number of stitches.

Work a provisional cast-on as the long-tail cast-on, but use waste yarn over your thumb.

When you are ready to graft, use fine-pointed scissors to clip the waste yarn out of each stitch, and place each resulting loop on a needle.

Another provisional cast-on is made with a loose crochet chain. Using contrasting waste yarn, crochet a chain with the desired number of stitches. Tie a small knot at the end of the chain to mark which end to pull from when the knitting is completed. Using a knitting needle and the knitting yarn, pick up and knit stitches through the back loops of the chain. Knit the pattern as usual and then loosen the contrasting thread, beginning at the knotted end. Gently pull out *one stitch at a time* and place the live stitches on a knitting needle.

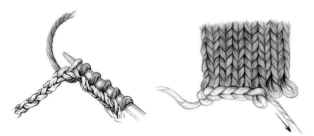

Pick up and knit stitches through back loops of the chain. Pull out the crochet chain to expose live stitches.

Slipping Stitches (sl)

When instructed to slip an edge stitch, slip the stitch as if to *knit*. This maneuver creates a nice firm edge for attaching to a piece of fabric or other knitting.

If you're directed to slip a stitch in the middle of a row, slip the stitch as if to *purl*. This maneuver moves the stitch into the correct position for the next step.

> **Tip**
> When moving stitches from one needle to another to correct a mistake or transfer stitches, slip them as if to *purl*. This leaves the stitches in the correct position for the next row. Slipping as if to purl does not twist the stitches as does slipping as if to knit.

Decreasing

Slip 1, Knit 1, Pass the Slipped Stitch Over (Sl 1 as if to knit, k1, psso) makes a left-slanting decrease.

Slip, Slip, Knit (ssk) is also a left-slanting decrease. Slip two stitches, one at a time, as if to knit,

insert the left needle through these two stitches, and knit them together through the back loops.

Slip 1, Knit 2 Together, Pass the Slipped Stitch Over (sl 1, k2tog, psso) decreases two stitches.

Binding Off (BO)

To prevent the bind-off edge from being too tight, bind off with a larger needle.

Lace Bind-Off When only part of a row needs to be bound off, knit two stitches together, *slip the last stitch worked back onto the left needle, and then knit the next two stitches together. Repeat from * for the required number of stitches. Pull out on the knitting to ensure that the bound-off stitches are not too tight. This method creates an edge similar to the selvedge edge of knitting.

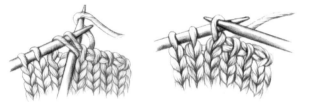

Knit two stitches together. Slip the stitch just worked back onto the left needle.

Binding Off in the Middle of a Row When binding off a few stitches in the middle of a row, use the lace bind-off. For a point or curved border on lace, this makes a smooth edge that looks more like the corresponding edge.

Some patterns call for a third type of bind-off that is worked off the left needle. Lift a specified number of stitches up and over the first stitch on the left needle. Then knit the last remaining stitch to finish off the row.

Lift the specified number of stitches over the first stitch on the left needle.

Through Back Loop (tbl)

Knitting through the back loop twists a stitch.

Single Crochet (sc)

This stitch is worked into hemstitched fabric. Insert crochet hook from front to back into one hemstitch hole, yarn over, pull loop to front of fabric, yarn over, and pull through the loop on the hook. *Insert the hook into the next hole in the fabric, yarn over, pull loop to front of fabric, yarn over, and pull through both loops on the hook. Repeat from * for desired length. Join with a slip stitch.

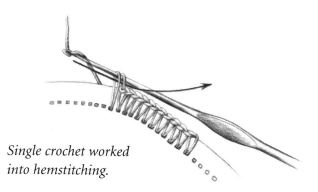

Single crochet worked into hemstitching.

READING PATTERNS

Read a lace knitting pattern like any other knitting pattern. Parentheses denote stitches that are to be repeated a specific number of times. For example, "(yo, k2tog) 3 times" is just a shorter way of saying "yo, k2tog, yo, k2tog, yo, k2tog."

READING CHARTS

Many knitters prefer to work from charts. Each stitch is represented by a square, and each square is annotated with a symbol that represents the way to work that stitch. Unless otherwise specified, read charts from bottom to top. When working back and forth in rows, read the first and all subsequent odd-numbered (right-side) rows from right to left. Read all even-numbered (wrong-side) rows from left to right. When working in the round, all rows are right-side rows and should be read from right to left.

> **Tip**
> If you pick up a project that has been sitting for some time, you may find that the stitches on the needles have stretched out a bit. To prevent this loose row from distorting the lace, rip out a row or two, and then begin knitting again.

RETRIEVING DROPPED STITCHES

Dropped stitches can be very difficult to retrieve in lace knitting. If you do drop a stitch, immediately relax your hands so that you don't pull outward on the knitting and cause the stitch to run. Place a pin or another needle through the loose stitch to hold it, and then rip out the knitting stitch by stitch until you can pick up the dropped stitch. Though tedious and slow, this process ensures that all the stitches and yarn-overs will be on the needle in the correct knitting position.

MISSED YARN-OVERS

If you lose a yarn-over or forget to put one in, you don't have to rip out your knitting to replace it. A yarn-over is actually the running thread between two stitches that gets looped over the right needle as the knitting progresses. If you forget to do a yarn-over, or it falls off while you're working the next row, you can retrieve it. Insert the left knitting needle from front to back under the thread that connects two stitches. If the knitting is not too tight, you will be able to see and pick up the thread quite easily. Then knit or purl it as directed in the instructions. This maneuver can cause the stitches to the right and left of the yarn-over to tighten. If you notice this happening, rip back to the missing yarn-over and correct the error.

JOINING THREAD

Because it is difficult to hide thread ends in the middle of a lace pattern, join new balls of thread at the edge of the knitting. Leaving a 4"- (10-cm) tail of the new yarn, tie the two yarns into a square knot, pulling the knot gently but firmly against the edge of the knitting. Leave the two tails hanging and continue knitting. Once you've finished the lace, work the tails into the wrong side of the fabric.

GRAFTING LIVE STITCHES TO LIVE STITCHES

Use grafting to join two sets of stitches together in such a way that the knitting appears seamless. In lace, this is usually the first, or cast-on, row of stitches and the last row of stitches. The stitches must be cast on with a provisional method (see page 15) and the final row must not be bound off, so that there are live stitches at both ends of the piece.

Set-Up for Grafting Carefully remove the waste yarn from the cast-on edge and place the exposed live stitches on a spare needle. Both ends of the knitting will be on needles. Hold both needles in your left hand with the right-side of the work facing outward. If possible, use the tail of yarn from the cast-on row for grafting. Thread this tail onto a tapestry needle of the appropriate size. Keep the grafting yarn below the knitting needles and work the stitches on the needles from right to left.

> **Tip**
> Pick up the live stitches from the invisible cast-on with a double-pointed needle so you won't have to worry about which direction the needle tip faces.

Garter Stitch Hold the two needles in your left hand with the wrong sides together as shown on page 19. (The purl bumps of the stitches on the needle nearest you (front needle) face toward you and the purl bumps on the needle farthest from you (back needle) face away from you.)

Set-up: Bring the tapestry needle through the first stitch on the front needle as if to *purl* and leave the stitch on the needle. Then bring the tapestry needle through the first stitch on the back needle as if to *purl* and leave that stitch on the needle.

Step 1: Bring the tapestry needle through the same stitch on the front needle as if to *knit* and then slip this stitch off the needle. Bring the tapestry needle through the next stitch on the front needle as if to *purl* and leave the stitch on the needle.

Step 2: Bring the tapestry needle through the first stitch on the back needle as if to *knit*, slip that stitch off the needle, and then bring the tapestry needle through the next stitch on the back needle as if to *purl* and leave the stitch on the needle. Repeat Steps 1 and 2 until no stitches remain on the needles, taking care to keep the tension on the grafting yarn the same as that of the knitting. Note that you will work only the first part of each step on the last stitch of each needle.

Here's a short cut.

Set-up: Near needle, purl. Far needle, purl. Leave both stitches on needles.

Step 1: Near needle, knit and slip off needle, purl.

Step 2: Far needle, knit and slip off needle, purl.

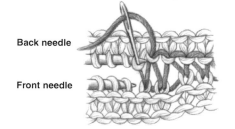

Grafting live stitches to live stitches in garter stitch.

Stockinette Stitch Hold the two needles in your left hand so that the right side of the knitting faces outward.

Set-up: Bring the tapestry needle through the first stitch on the front needle as if to *purl* and leave the stitch on the needle. Then bring the tapestry needle through the first stitch on the back needle as if to *knit* and leave that stitch on the needle.

Step 1: Bring the tapestry needle through the same stitch on the front needle as if to *knit* and then slip the stitch off the needle. Bring the tapestry needle through the next stitch on the front needle as if to *purl* and leave the stitch on the needle.

Step 2: Bring the tapestry needle through the first stitch on the back needle as if to *purl,* slip the stitch off the needle, and then bring the tapestry needle through the next stitch on the back needle as if to *knit* and leave the stitch on the needle.

Repeat Steps 1 and 2 until no stitches remain on the needles, taking care to keep the tension on the grafting yarn the same as that of the knitting. Note that you will work only the first part of each step on the last stitch of each needle.

Here's a short-cut.

Set-up: Near needle, purl. Far needle, knit. Leave both stitches on needles.

Step 1: Near needle, knit and slip off needle, purl.

Step 2: Far needle, purl and slip off needle, knit.

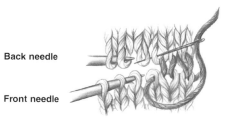

Grafting live stitches to live stitches in stockinette stitch.

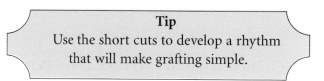

Tip
Use the short cuts to develop a rhythm that will make grafting simple.

GRAFTING A CAST-ON EDGE TO LIVE STITCHES

Garter Stitch Hold the needle with the live stitches in your left hand with the right side of the knitting facing you. Fold the knitting so that the cast-on edge is on top and even with the needle. Working from right to left, bring the threaded tapestry needle under the first stitch of the cast-on edge, *bring the tapestry needle through the first stitch on the needle as if to *knit*, and slip the stitch off the needle. Then bring the tapestry needle through the next stitch on the needle as if to *purl* and leave the stitch on the needle. Bring the tapestry needle back down through the same stitch of the cast-on edge, from the top, and then up through the next cast-on stitch. Repeat from * until no stitches remain.

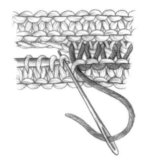

Grafting cast-on edge to live stitches in garter stitch.

Stockinette Stitch Hold the needle with the live stitches in your left hand so that the right side of the knitting faces you. Fold the cast-on edge behind the knitting and even with the needle. Working from right to left, bring the tapestry needle up under the first stitch of the cast-on edge and then through the first stitch on the needle as if to *purl*. *Bring the tapestry needle back down through the same stitch on the cast-on edge and up under the next cast-on stitch. Bring it through the first stitch on the needle as if to *knit*, slip the stitch off the needle, bring the tapestry needle through the next stitch on the needle as if to *purl*, and leave the stitch on the needle. Repeat from * until no stitches remain.

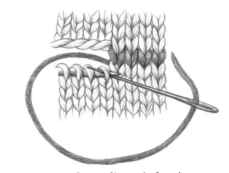

Grafting cast-on edge to live stitches in stockinette stitch.

COMBINING FABRIC AND KNITTED LACE

Purchased fabric can be cut to size, finished off, and then edged with a knitted border. This technique is particularly useful for making bath and table linens. When purchasing a piece of fabric to attach lace to, consider the thickness and weight of the piece. Although many fabrics are suitable for lace borders, linen needlework fabric is ideal—it's heavy enough to support the knitting and will block out flat once the border is complete. If the fabric is very light, a small thin border should be attached to prevent puckering or distorting the edge.

Linen doily rounds, handkerchiefs, and fingertip towels are good beginner projects. Some commercially-available linen rounds and handkerchiefs are hemstitched, a hemming process that results in small holes near the edge. These hard-to-find items are mostly available in fine-linen or antique stores and by mail order and are ideal foundations for lace borders—you can work a row of single crochet into the holes and then knit or sew the border onto this foundation.

Preparing Fabric for a Lace Edging I use one of two methods to finish cut fabric. Either I handstitch a small rolled hem or run the edge through a serger. I then attach the lace by hand-sewing it on top of or just above the hem or serged edge.

I also sometimes work a row of slip-stitch crochet into the fabric about 1/4" in from the edge, above the hem or serging. Use a very small crochet hook that will accommodate the thread and not tear a hole in the fabric. Insert the hook into the fabric from front to back, yarn over the hook, and pull it gently through the fabric. Working about 1/4" in from the edge in a straight line, *reinsert the hook into the fabric about 1/16 to 1/8" from the last stitch, yarn over and pull through fabric and loop on hook. Repeat from * around edge of fabric. *Note:* The yarn will always be pulled from the wrong to the right side of the fabric. The slip stitch will look like a small chain on top of the fabric. The stitches should be no larger than 1/8". Larger stitches will cause the fabric to pucker and the lace border will not lie flat.

To finish off, work the last stitch and pull the yarn end through the loop. Thread the end on a tapestry needle and run the needle under the chain formed by the first stitch. Insert the needle into the hole the thread is coming out of in the last stitch and pull

through to the wrong side. Weave the end under the stitches on the wrong side.

Attaching Lace to Fabric To sew a lace border to a piece of fabric, pin the lace to the border using knitter's safety pins or straight pins. Equally distribute the lace around the edge of the fabric. This can be done by folding the piece of fabric into quarters, marking with pins and then folding the lace into quarters and marking. Pin together at the markings.

Using a sewing or tapestry needle that will accommodate the same thread used for the knitting, overcast the two edges together, gently stretching the lace as necessary. Sew into the "bump" produced by the garter stitch of the lace, and then into the stitch

Insert hook into fabric and wrap thread over hook.

Pull loop through fabric and loop already on hook.

Thread the end on a tapestry needle and run the needle under the chain formed by the first stitch.

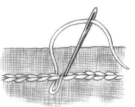

Rolled hem.

Serged edge.

Slip-stitch crochet worked into fabric.

produced by the single crochet or slip stitches. If the fabric doesn't have a crocheted edge, sew the lace directly to the fabric with small stitches.

Attaching a Border as it is Knitted When attaching a knitted border as it is knitted to a row of slip-stitch or to a single crochet edge, knit together the last stitch of every other row, or rows that end at the crocheted edge, with a crochet chain. Do this by slipping the last stitch, inserting the needle into the chain and picking up and knitting a stitch, then passing the slipped stitch over.

In order to knit an edge that fits your project exactly and ends with the last row of a repeat, you may have to knit into some chain stitches twice or skip a few chain stitches. To determine how many stitches to use twice or skip, do some simple calculations.

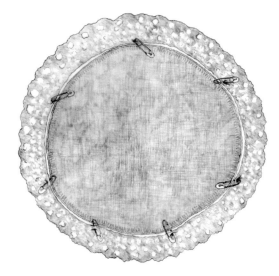

Pin lace to fabric with knitter's safety pins.

Sew lace to crochet edge on fabric.

Slip the last stitch.

Pick up and knit a stitch through the crochet chain.

Pass the slipped stitch over.

Attaching a border as it is knitted to a row of slip-stitch crochet.

Attach a border as it is knitted to a single-crochet edge in the same way.

Divide half the number of rows in a repeat into the number of crochet chains on the edge. The result is the number of repeats that will fit and the chains left over. For example, say the lace border you want to use has 18 rows in a repeat and you have 122 chain stitches to attach it to. For every 18 rows of lace, 9 will be attached to the crocheted edge. Divide 122 by 9 to get 13 repeats with a remainder of 5. To work 14 full repeats, you need 4 more chain stitches. By working 2 knit stitches into 1 chain stitch 4 times, the crocheted edge will accommodate 14 full repeats of the lace pattern. Distribute these 4 "doubled-up" stitches evenly around the edge.

Another way to make the border fit is by knitting 13 repeats and skipping 5 chain stitches. Again, evenly distribute the 5 skipped stitches around the edge.

Working Around Corners To knit a border around square corners, such as for a handkerchief, use the "doubled-up" stitches method. If your lace has a 12-row repeat, work as usual to within 12 chain stitches from the corner, then use each of these next 12 chains twice, and do the same for the next 12 chain stitches on the other side of the corner. The lace will be full enough to go around the corner and lie flat when blocked.

BLOCKING AND FINISHING

All borders knitted with cotton thread require blocking or stretching for the lace pattern to show. Because cotton thread retains its blocked shape, starch is generally unnecessary.

Blocking Supplies
•Stainless Steel T-pins or Clover Blocking Pins
•1"-to 2"-thick upholstery foam covered with 1" gingham (to provide a grid for pinning out), or other padded surface
•Blocking wire or small knitting needle, size 0
•Spray bottle with water

A separate border which you attach to a piece should fit the edge when slightly stretched. Cotton thread will stretch when wet and pinned out.

If you attach borders to fabric as you knit, or if you sew them to fabric, the whole piece will require blocking. This often smoothes out the fabric as well, so no ironing will be necessary. If you're blocking a border before attaching it to the fabric, be careful that you block it to the piece's measurements.

Step 1: Wet the entire piece in warm water, adding mild soap if it has become soiled from handling. Gently swish the piece around in the water until it is completely saturated. Rinse thoroughly and then roll in a towel to blot out excess moisture. Do not twist or wring. Lace knitted on thread finer than size 70 should be thoroughly dried before blocking; otherwise the stitches may break when you pin it out.

Step 2: Block by placing the lace on the padded surface and pinning it to size. To ensure that you're pinning a doily to the correct size, draw a circle on the padded surface the desired finished doily diameter. You can pin out very large pieces on a bed or carpeted floor covered with fabric or a sheet.

Step 3: Gently stretch the lace border (and fabric, if it is attached), pinning out each corner and each point. Adjust the pins as necessary for even stretching. If the piece begins to dry before you've pinned it all out, dampen it with a spray bottle. Be sure there is plenty of circulating air, and no direct sunlight on the lace as it dries. Allow the lace to dry *completely* before removing the pins.

When you're blocking straight, flat pieces, a

blocking wire helps. Insert the wire into the top edge of the knitting or into the holes of the lace close to the straight edge. If you don't use a blocking wire, it is difficult to pin the straight edge out so it does not ripple or look wavy when the pins are removed. If blocking wires are not available, use a long straight knitting needle size 0 or smaller.

Clover Blocking Pins are actually two pins joined together with a plastic top, and they have a slight curve to them. They are very good for blocking the straight edges of doilies and will prevent a rippling or wavy affect. Place the pins under the blocking wire to keep it straight and secure as you are stretching and pinning the bottom edges of the lace.

CARING FOR LACE

Washing lace by hand before it gets too dirty is the best way to keep it looking new and fresh. Wash with a mild soap such as Ivory Flakes and warm water. A mild solution of lemon juice, hydrogen peroxide, or nonchlorine bleach is fairly safe for stains. Each time you wash a piece, repeat the blocking procedure. If ironing is necessary, lay the lace face down on a thick terry towel and press gently.

Storing Lace To store lace, wrap it in acid-free tissue paper. If the piece is large, such as a tablecloth, fold it around tissue paper and place it in an acid-free storage box. When tissue paper is tucked into the folds, there will be no wrinkles.

Doilies or handkerchiefs stored long-term should be rolled over a cardboard tube (such as a paper-towel roll). Cover the roll with acid-free tissue paper and gently roll the lace over, then cover the lace with another layer of tissue paper. If you have many pieces, attach a written description to the outside of each roll. As with any textile, your pieces should be kept out of direct sunlight in a cool dark environment.

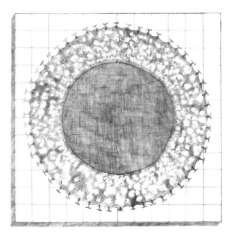

Use T-pins or Clover Blocking Pins to block lace on a padded surface covered with gingham.

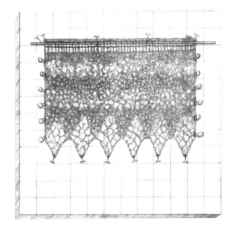

Use a blocking wire for a straight edge bordered with holes. Use Clover Blocking Pins for other straight edges.

Abbreviations

beg	begin; beginning	rem	remains; remaining
bet	between	rep	repeat
BO	bind off	rnd(s)	round(s)
cm	centimeter(s)	RS	right side
CO	cast on	sc	single crochet
cont	continue; continuing	sl	slip
dec(s)	decrease(s); decreasing	ssk	slip 2 stitches (1 at a time), knit these 2
dpn	double-pointed needle(s)		stitches together through back loops
foll	following	st(s)	stitch(es)
g	gram(s)	St st	stockinette stitch
inc	increase(s); increasing	tbl	through back loop
k	knit	tog	together
kwise	knitwise	WS	wrong side
m	marker	wyb	with yarn in back
MC	main color	wyf	with yarn in front
mm	millimeter(s)	yo	yarn over
p	purl	*	repeat starting point (i.e., repeat from *)
patt	pattern	(); []	instructions that are to be worked as a
pwise	purlwise		group a specified number of times
psso	pass slipped stitch over		

Chart Symbols

□	k on RS; p on WS	V	sl 1 wyb
·	p on RS; k on WS	∕	k3tog
/	k2tog on RS and WS	\	p3tog
\	ssk on RS and WS	b	k1 tbl
O	yo	∧	sl2 tog kwise, k1, p2sso
◉	place rem st after BO on left needle, yo	⋋	sl 1, k2tog, psso
◯	drop yo on next row	∕	p2tog

∕2	k2tog, sl this st back to left needle, pass the last 2 sts over the first st, place st back on right needle	⋎4	(k1, p1, k1, p1) in same st
∕5	Skip first st, pass next 5 sts on left needle over first st, k2tog	⋎5	(k1, p1, k1, p1, k1) in same st
∕6	pass last 6 sts on left needle over first st on left needle	▩	no st
∕7	k3tog, k4tog; pass 1st dec over 2nd dec	▪	st left on right needle after BO
∕10	pass last 10 sts on left needle over first st on left needle	⌒	bind off
∕16	pass 16 sts on left needle over first st on left needle		

④ ④ ④ ④ ④ ④ ④ ④

sl 8 sts to right needle, elongating them, sl them back to left needle, pass the last 4 sts over the first 4 and knit these 8 sts in that order

LACE PATTERNS

Here are Blanche's patterns written in today's abbreviations and charted. I have given the stitch numbers at the end of the rows when they differ from the previous row. If no stitch number is given, the number hasn't changed.

Knitted Lace #1

CO 12 sts.

Set-up row: Knit.

Row 1: Sl 1, k1, yo, k2tog, k3, k2tog, yo, k1, yo, k2—13 sts.

Row 2 and all even-numbered rows: Knit.

Row 3: Sl 1, k1, yo, k2tog, k2, k2tog, yo, k3, yo, k2—14 sts.

Row 5: Sl 1, k1, yo, k2tog, k1, k2tog, yo, k5, yo, k2—15 sts.

Row 7: Sl 1, k1, yo, k2tog, k3, yo, k2tog, k1, k2tog, yo, k2tog, k1—14 sts.

Row 9: Sl 1, k1, yo, k2tog, k4, yo, sl 1, k2tog, psso, yo, k2tog, k1—13 sts.

Row 11: Sl 1, k1, yo, k2tog, k4, k2tog, yo, k2tog, k1—12 sts.

Repeat Rows 1–12 for desired length. BO on Row 12.

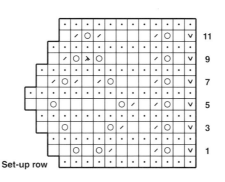

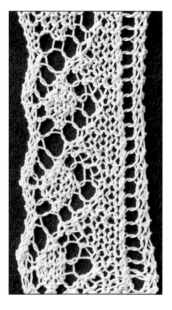

Heart Lace #1

CO 15 sts.

Set-up row: Knit.

Row 1: K9, p1, yo, k1, yo, p1, k3—17 sts.

Row 2: K4, p3, k3, yo twice, k2tog, k5—18 sts.

Row 3: K7, p1, k2, p1, k1, [yo, k1] 2 times, p1, k3—20 sts.

Row 4: K4, p5, k11.

Row 5: K10, p1, k2, yo, k1, yo, k2, p1, k3—22 sts.

Row 6: K4, p7, k3, [yo twice, k2tog] 2 times, k4—24 sts.

Row 7: K6, [p1, k2] 2 times, p1, k7, p1, k3.

26

Row 8: K4, p7, k13.

Row 9: K12, p1, ssk, k3, k2tog, p1, k3—22 sts.

Row 10: K4, p5, k3, [yo twice, k2tog] 3 times, k4—25 sts.

Row 11: K6, [p1, k2] 3 times, p1, ssk, k1, k2tog, p1, k3—23 sts.

Row 12: K4, p3, k16.

Row 13: K15, p1, sl 1, k2tog, psso, p1, k3—21 sts.

Rows 14 and 15: Knit.

Row 16: BO 6 sts, knit to end—15 sts.

Repeat Rows 1–16 for desired length. BO on Row 1

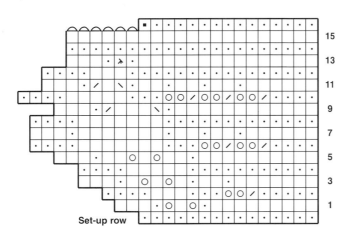

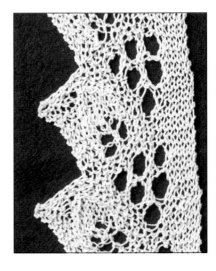

Hearth and Home Lace

CO 10 sts.

Set-up row: Knit.

Row 1: Sl 1, k1, yo, p2tog, k2, yo twice, k2tog, k2—11 sts.

Row 2: K4, p1, k2, yo, p2tog, k2.

Row 3: Sl 1, k1, yo, p2tog, k3, yo twice, k2tog, k2—12 sts.

Row 4: K4, p1, k3, yo, p2tog, k2.

Row 5: Sl 1, k1, yo, p2tog, k4, yo twice, k2tog, k2—13 sts.

Row 6: K4, p1, k4, yo, p2tog, k2.

Row 7: Sl 1, k1, yo, p2tog, k9.

Row 8: BO 3, k5, yo, p2tog, k2—10 sts.

Repeat Rows 1–8 for desired length. BO on Row 8.

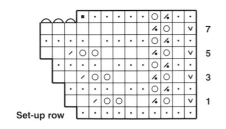

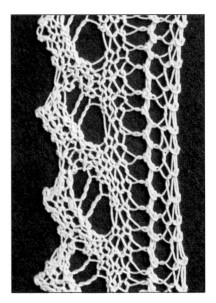

Mrs. Belli's Diamond Edging

CO 9 sts.

Set-up row: Knit.

Row 1: K3, [k2tog, yo] 2 times, k1, yo, k1—10 sts.

Row 2: [K1, p1] 3 times, k4.

Row 3: K2, [k2tog, yo] 2 times, k3, yo, k1—11 sts.

Row 4: K1, p1, k3, p1, k1, p1, k3.

Row 5: K1, [k2tog, yo] 2 times, k5, yo, k1—12 sts.

Row 6: K1, p1, k5, p1, k1, p1, k2.

Row 7: K3, [yo, k2tog] 2 times, k1, k2tog, yo, k2tog—11 sts.

Row 8: K1, p1, k3, p1, k1, p1, k3.

Row 9: K4, yo, k2tog, yo, k3tog, yo, k2tog—10 sts.

Row 10: [K1, p1] 3 times, k4.

Row 11: K5, yo, k3tog, yo, k2tog— 9 sts.

Row 12: [K1, p1] 2 times, k5.

Repeat Rows 1–12 for desired length. BO in knit after Row 12.

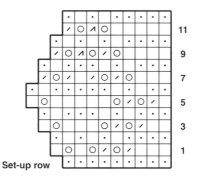

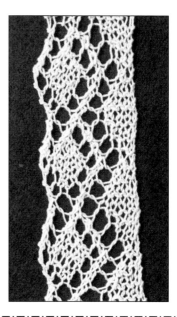

Narrow Knitted Edging

CO 9 sts.

Set-up row: Knit.

Row 1: K3, yo, [k2tog, yo twice] 2 times, k2tog—11 sts.

Row 2: [K2, p1] 2 times, k2, yo, k2tog, k1.

Row 3: K3, yo, k2tog, k6.

Row 4: K8, yo, k2tog, k1.

Row 5: K3, yo, k2tog, k2, [yo twice, k2tog] 2 times—13 sts.

Row 6: [K2, p1] 2 times, k4, yo, k2tog, k1.

Row 7: K3, yo, k2tog, k8.

Row 8: K10, yo, k2tog, k1.

Row 9: K3, yo, k2tog, k4, [yo twice, k2tog] 2 times—15 sts.

Row 10: [K2, p1] 2 times, k6, yo, k2tog, k1.

Row 11: K3, yo, k2tog, k10.

Row 12: BO 6, k5, yo, k2tog, k1— 9 sts.

Repeat Rows 1–12 for desired length. BO on Row 12.

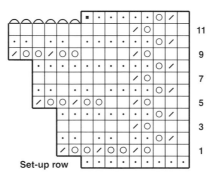

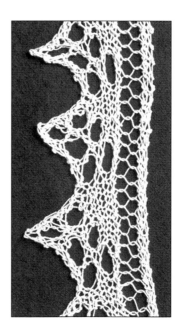

Smilax Lace

CO 15 sts.

Set-up row: Knit.

Row 1: Sl 1, k1, yo, k2tog, k3, [k2tog, yo] 2 times, [k1, yo] 2 times, p2tog—16 sts.

Row 2 and all even-numbered rows: YO, p2tog, purl to end.

Row 3: Sl 1, k2, yo, k2tog, k1, [k2tog, yo] 2 times, k3, yo, k1, yo, p2tog—17 sts.

Row 5: Sl 1, k3, yo, sl 1, k2tog, psso, yo, k2tog, yo, k5, yo, k1, yo, p2tog—18 sts.

Row 7: Sl 1, k4, yo, sl 1, k2tog, psso, yo, k7, yo, k1, yo, p2tog—19 sts.

Row 9: Sl 1, k2, k2tog, yo, k1, [yo, k2tog] 2 times, k3, [k2tog, yo] 2 times, p2tog—18 sts.

Row 11: Sl 1, k1, k2tog, yo, k3, [yo, k2tog] 2 times, k1, [k2tog, yo] 2 times, p2tog—17 sts.

Row 13: Sl 1, k2tog, yo, k5, yo, k2tog, yo, sl 1, k2tog, psso, yo, k2tog, yo, p2tog—16 sts.

Row 15: K2tog, yo, k7, yo, sl 1, k2tog, psso, yo, k2tog, yo, p2tog—15 sts.

Repeat Rows 1–16. BO on Row 16.

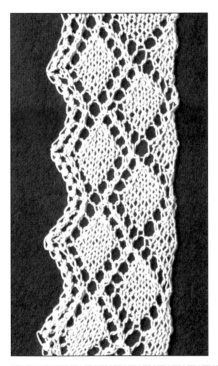

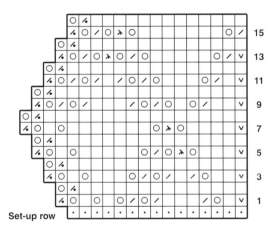

New Palm Leaf Edging

CO 11 sts.

Set-up row: Knit.

Row 1: K3, yo, k2tog, yo twice, k2tog, k2, yo twice, p2tog—13 sts.

Row 2: YO, p2tog, k5, p1, k5.

Row 3: K4, yo, k5, yo twice, k2tog, yo twice, p2tog—16 sts.

Row 4: YO, p2tog, k3, p1, k10.

Row 5: K5, yo, k3, yo twice, k2tog, k4, yo twice, p2tog—19 sts.

Row 6: YO, p2tog, k7, p1, k9.

Row 7: K6, yo, k9, k2tog, yo, p2tog.

Rows 8, 10, 12, and 14: YO, p2tog, knit to end.

Row 9: K7, yo, k2tog, k6, k2tog, yo, p2tog—18 sts.

Row 11: K8, yo, k2tog, k4, k2tog, yo, p2tog—17 sts.

Row 13: K9, yo, [k2tog] 3 times,

yo, p2tog—15 sts.

Row 15: K8, k2tog, yo, k3tog, p2tog—12 sts.

Row 16: YO, p2tog, k2tog, k8—11 sts.

Repeat Rows 1–16 for desired length. BO on Row 16.

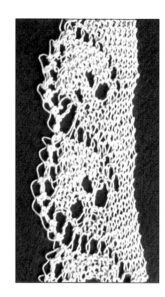

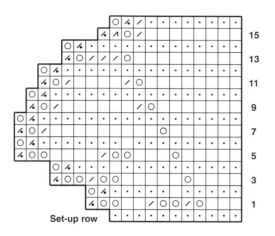

Clover Leaf Lace

CO 10 sts.

Set-up row: Knit.

Row 1: K2, yo, p2tog, k1, yo twice, k2tog, k3—11 sts.

Row 2: K5, p1, k1, yo, p2tog, k2.

Row 3: K2, yo, p2tog, k7.

Row 4: K8, yo, p2tog, k1.

Row 5: K2, yo, p2tog, k1, [yo twice, k2tog] 2 times, k2—13 sts.

Row 6: K4, p1, k2, p1, k1, yo, p2tog, k2.

Row 7: K2, yo, p2tog, k9.

Row 8: BO 3, k6, yo, p2tog, k1— 10 sts.

Repeat Rows 1–8 for desired length. BO on Row 8.

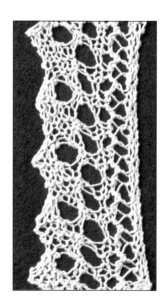

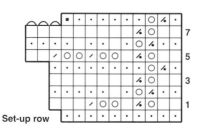

Hilton Lace

CO 17 sts.

Set-up row: Knit.

Row 1: K2, yo, k2tog, k4, yo, k3tog, [k1, yo] 2 times, k2tog, yo, k2—18 sts.

Row 2 and all even-numbered rows: YO, k2tog, knit to end.

Row 3: K7, yo, k3tog, k1, yo, k3, yo, k2tog, yo, k2—19 sts.

Row 5: K2, yo, k2tog, k2, yo, k3tog, k1, yo, k5, yo, k2tog, yo, k2—20 sts.

Row 7: K5, yo, k3tog, k1, yo, k7, yo, k2tog, yo, k2—21 sts.

Row 9: K2, yo, k2tog, k8, yo, k3tog, k1, [yo, k2tog] 2 times, k1—20 sts.

Row 11: K11, yo, k3tog, k1, [yo, k2tog] 2 times, k1—19 sts.

Row 13: K2, yo, k2tog, k6, yo, k3tog, k1, [yo, k2tog] 2 times, k1—18 sts.

Row 15: K9, yo, k3tog, k1, [yo, k2tog] 2 times, k1—17 sts.

Repeat Rows 1–16 for desired length. BO in knit after Row 16.

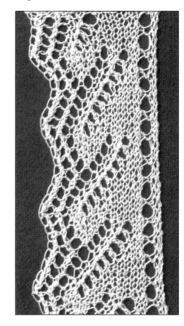

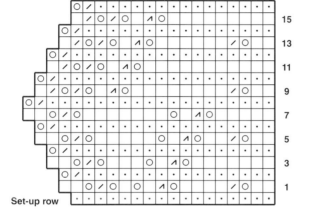

Fan Lace #1

CO 12 sts.

Set-up row: Knit.

Row 1: Sl 1, k1, yo twice, k2tog, k4, k2tog, yo, k2—13 sts.

Row 2: YO, k2tog, k8, p1, k2.

Row 3: Sl 1, k8, k2tog, yo, k2.

Rows 4 and 8: YO, k2tog, knit to end.

Row 5: Sl 1, k1, [yo twice, k2tog] 2 times, k3, k2tog, yo, k2—15 sts.

Row 6: YO, k2tog, k7, [p1, k2] 2 times.

Row 7: Sl 1, k10, k2tog, yo, k2.

Row 9: Sl 1, k1, [yo twice, k2tog] 3 times, k3, k2tog, yo, k2—18 sts.

Row 10: YO, k2tog, k7, [p1, k2] 3 times.

Row 11: Sl 1, k10, skip first st, pass

last 5 sts on left needle over first st, k2tog—12 sts.

Row 12: YO, k2tog, k10.

Repeat Rows 1–12 for desired length. BO in knit after Row 12.

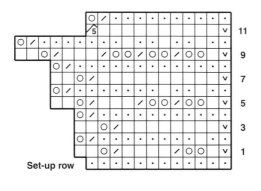

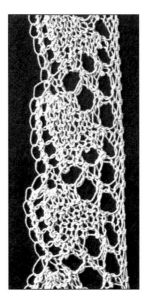

Fairy Lace

CO 12 sts.

Set-up row: Knit.

Row 1: [YO, p2tog] 2 times, k1, [yo twice, k2tog] 3 times, k1—15 sts.

Row 2: K3, [p1, k2] 2 times, p1, k1, [yo, p2tog] 2 times—15 sts.

Row 3: [YO, p2tog] 2 times, k11.

Row 4: BO 3, k7, [yo, p2tog] 2 times—12 sts.

Repeat Rows 1–4 for desired length. BO in knit after Row 4.

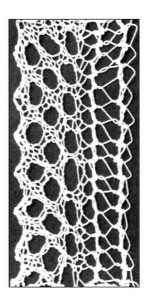

Imitation Torchon Lace

CO 11 sts.

Set-up row: Knit.

Row 1: Sl 1, k8, yo, k2—12 sts.

Rows 2, 4, and 6: Knit.

Row 3: Sl 1, k7, yo, k2tog, yo, k2—13 sts.

Row 5: Sl 1, k6, [yo, k2tog] 2 times, yo, k2—14 sts.

Row 7: Sl 1, k2, k2tog, yo twice, k2tog, k1, [yo, k2tog] 2 times, yo, k2—15 sts.

Rows 8 and 12: K10, p1, k4.

Row 9: Sl 1, [k2tog, yo twice, k2tog] 2 times, [yo, k2tog] 2 times, yo, k2—16 sts.

Row 10: K9, p1, k3, p1, k2.

Row 11: Sl 1, k2, k2tog, yo twice, k2tog, ssk, [yo, k2tog] 3 times, k1—15 sts.

Row 13: Sl 1, k5, ssk, [yo, k2tog] 3 times, k1—14 sts.

Rows 14, 16, 18, and 20: Knit.

Row 15: Sl 1, k6, ssk, [yo, k2tog] 2 times, k1—13 sts.

Row 17: Sl 1, k7, ssk, yo, k2tog, k1—12 sts.

Row 19: Sl 1, k8, k2tog, k1—11 sts.

Repeat Rows 1–20 for desired length. BO on Row 20.

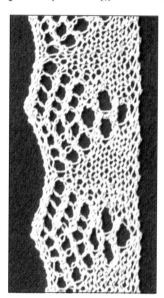

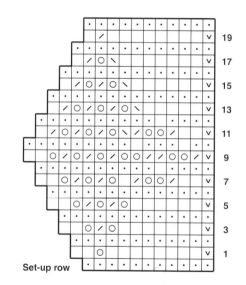

Diamond Edge Lace

CO 12 sts.

Set-up row: Knit.

Row 1: Sl 1, k1, yo, k2tog, yo, k8—13 sts.

Rows 2, 4, 6, 8, and 10: Knit.

Row 3: Sl 1, k1, yo, k2tog, k1, yo, k8—14 sts.

Row 5: Sl 1, k1, [yo, k2tog] 2 times, yo, k8—15 sts.

Row 7: Sl 1, k1, yo, k2tog, k1, yo, k2tog, yo, k8—16 sts.

Row 9: Sl 1, k1, [yo, k2tog] 3

times, yo, k8—17 sts.

Row 11: Sl 1, k1, yo, k2tog, k1, [yo, k2tog] 2 times, yo, k8—18 sts.

Row 12: BO 6 sts, k11—12 sts. Repeat Rows 1–12 for desired length. BO on Row 12.

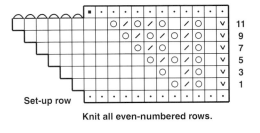

Set-up row

Knit all even-numbered rows.

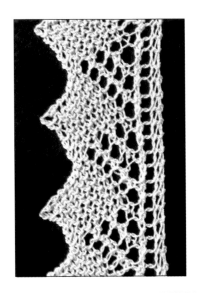

Fan Lace #2

CO 13 sts.

Set-up row: Knit.

Row 1: K11, yo twice, k2—15 sts.

Row 2: K2, [k1, p1, k1, p1, k1] into "yo twice", p7, k4—18 sts.

Row 3: K3, ssk, k13—17 sts.

Rows 4, 6, 8, 10, and 12: K2, purl to last 4 sts, k4.

Row 5: K3, ssk, k5, [yo, k1] 5 times, yo, k2—22 sts.

Row 7: K3, ssk, k17—21 sts.

Row 9: K3, ssk, k3, [yo, k2tog] 6 times, k1—20 sts.

Row 11: K3, ssk, k15—19 sts.

Row 13: K3, ssk, [yo, k2tog] 6 times, yo, k2.

Rows 14 and 15: Knit.

Row 16: BO 6 sts, k12—13 sts. Repeat Rows 1–16 for desired length. BO on Row 16.

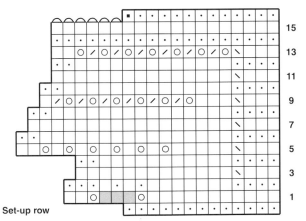

Set-up row

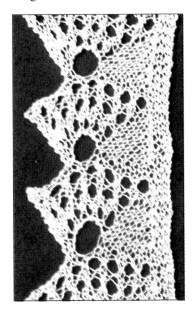

Pine Burr Lace

CO 10 sts.

Set-up row: Purl.

Row 1: Sl 1, k1, yo, p2tog, (k1, p1, k1, p1, k1) in next st, yo, p2tog, k1, yo twice, k2—16 sts.

Row 2: K3, p1, k1, yo, p2tog, k5, yo, p2tog, k2—16 sts.

Row 3: Sl 1, k1, [yo, p2tog, k5] 2 times.

Row 4: [K5, yo, p2tog] 2 times, k2.

Row 5: Sl 1, k1, yo, p2tog, k2tog, k1, k2tog, yo, p2tog, k5—14 sts.

Row 6: BO 2 sts, k2, yo, p2tog, k3tog, yo, p2tog, k2—10 sts.

Repeat Rows 1–6 for desired length. BO in purl after Row 6.

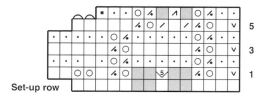

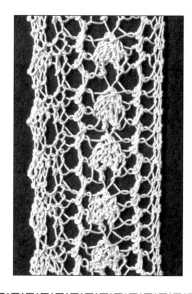

Narrow Knitted Lace

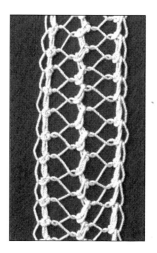

CO 6 sts.

Set-up row: Knit.

Row 1: [YO, p2tog] 3 times.

Row 2: [YO, p2tog] 3 times.

Repeat Rows 1 and 2 to desired length. BO all sts.

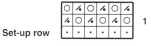

Point Lace

CO 19 sts.

Set-up row: Knit.

Row 1: Sl 1, k1, yo, p2tog, k2, yo, p2tog, k5, yo, k6—20 sts.

Rows 2, 4, and 6: Sl 1, knit to last 8 sts, [yo, p2tog, k2] 2 times.

Row 3: Sl 1, k1, yo, p2tog, k2, yo, p2tog, k8, [yo, k2] 2 times—22 sts.

Row 5: Sl 1, k1, yo, p2tog, k2, yo, p2tog, k5, yo, k9—23 sts.

Row 7: Sl 1, k1, yo, p2tog, k2, yo, p2tog, k15.

Row 8: BO 4, k10, [yo, p2tog, k2] 2 times—19 sts.

Repeat Rows 1–8 for desired length. BO in knit after Row 8.

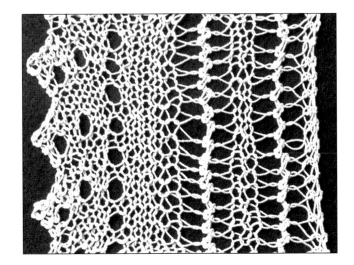

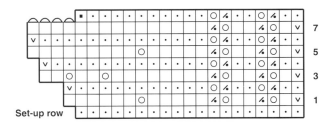

Hearth and Home Edging

CO 15 sts.

Set-up row: Knit.

Row 1: Sl 1, k2, [yo, k2tog] 2 times, k3, yo, k2tog, [yo] 3 times, k2tog, k1—17 sts.

Row 2: Sl 1, k2, p1, k3, yo, k2tog,

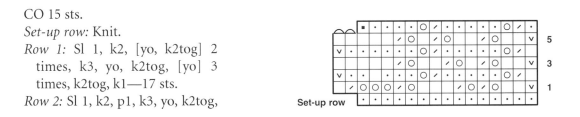

k5, yo, k2tog, k1.

Row 3: Sl 1, k2, yo, k2tog, k1, yo, k2tog, k2, yo, k2tog, k5.

Row 4: Sl 1, k6, yo, k2tog, k5, yo, k2tog, k1.

Row 5: Sl 1, [k2, yo, k2tog] 2 times, k1, yo, k2tog, k5.

Row 6: BO 2, k4, yo, k2tog, k5, yo, k2tog, k1—15 sts.

Repeat Rows 1–6 for desired length. BO in knit after Row 6.

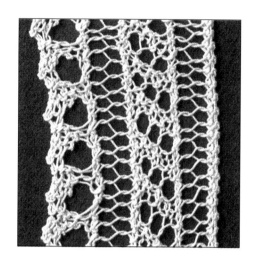

Normandy Lace

CO 15 sts.

Set-up row: Knit.

Row 1: K8, k2tog, yo, k3, yo, k2—16 sts.

Row 2: K2, yo, k5, yo, k2tog, k7—17 sts.

Row 3: K6, [k2tog, yo, k1] 2 times, yo, k2tog, k1, yo, k2—18 sts.

Row 4: K2, yo, k1, k2tog, yo, k3, yo, k2tog, k1, yo, k2tog, k5—19 sts.

Row 5: K4, k2tog, yo, k1, k2tog, yo, k5, yo, k2tog, k1, yo, k2—20 sts.

Row 6: K2, yo, k1, k2tog, yo, k3, yo, k2tog, k2, yo, k2tog, k1, yo, k2tog, k3—21 sts.

Row 7: K5, yo, k2tog, k1, yo,

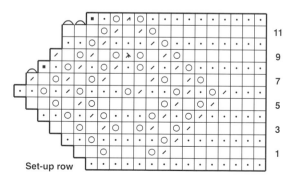

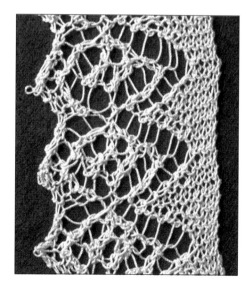

k2tog, k3, [k2tog, yo, k1] 2 times, k2tog—20 sts.

Row 8: BO 1, [k1, yo, k2tog] 3 times, k1, k2tog, yo, k6—19 sts.

Row 9: K7, yo, k2tog, k1, yo, sl 1, k2tog, psso, [yo, k1, k2tog] 2 times—18 sts.

Row 10: K2, yo, k2tog, k3, k2tog, yo, k8—17 sts.

Row 11: K9, yo, k2tog, k1, k2tog, yo, k3.

Row 12: BO 2, k1, yo, k3tog, yo, k10—15 sts.

Repeat Rows 1–12 for desired length. BO in knit after Row 12.

Mrs. Demming's Lace

CO 28 sts.

Set-up row: Purl.

Row 1: K3, k2tog, k2, yo, k1, [yo, k2tog] 2 times, yo, k2, k2tog, k4, k2tog, k2, yo, k1, yo, k2tog, yo, k1—29 sts.

Row 2 and all even-numbered rows: Purl.

Row 3: K2, k2tog, k2, yo, k3, [yo, k2tog] 2 times, yo, k2, [k2tog, k2] 2 times, yo, k3, yo, k2tog, yo, k1—30 sts.

Row 5: K1, k2tog, k2, yo, k5, [yo, k2tog] 2 times, yo, k2, k2tog twice, k2, yo, k5, yo, k2tog, yo, k1—31 sts.

Row 7: K6, k2tog, k2, yo, k2tog, [yo, k1] 2 times, yo, k2, k2tog, k2, k2tog, k1, k2tog, k2, [yo, k2tog] 2 times—30 sts.

Row 9: K5, k2tog, k2, [yo, k2tog] 2 times, yo, k3, yo, [k2, k2tog] 2 times, k2, [yo, k2tog] 2 times—29 sts.

Row 11: K4, k2tog, k2, [yo, k2tog] 2 times, yo, k5, yo, k2, k2tog twice, k2, [yo, k2tog] 2 times—28 sts.

Repeat Rows 1–12 for desired length. BO on Row 12.

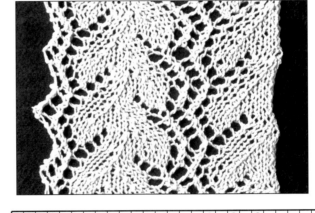

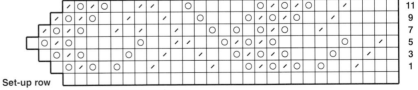

Set-up row

Purl all even-numbered rows.

Ladies' Home Journal Edging #1

CO 15 sts.

Set-up row: Knit.

Row 1: K3, yo, k2tog, k3, yo, k1, yo, k6—17 sts.

Row 2: K6, yo, k3, yo, k2tog, k3, yo, k2tog, k1—18 sts.

Row 3: K3, yo, k2tog twice, yo, k5, yo, k6—19 sts.

Row 4: BO 4, k1, yo, k2tog, k3,

k2tog, [yo, k2tog, k1] 2 times—
14 sts.

Row 5: K3, [yo, k2tog, k1] 2 times,

k2tog, yo, k3.

Row 6: K3, yo, k1, yo, sl 2, k1, p2sso, yo, k4, yo, k2tog, k1—15 sts.

Repeat Rows 1–6 for desired length. BO in knit after Row 6.

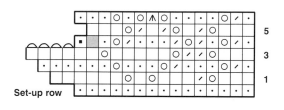

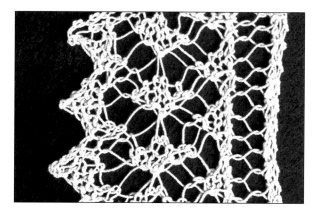

- -

Ladies' Home Journal Edging #2

CO 20 sts.

Set-up row: Knit.

Row 1: K3, yo, p2tog, k1, yo, k2tog, k2, yo, k2tog, k3, yo, p2tog, k1, [yo] 3 times, k2—23 sts.

Row 2: K3, p1, k2, yo, p2tog, k10, yo, p2tog, k3.

Row 3: K3, yo, p2tog, [k2, yo,

k2tog] 2 times, k2, yo, p2tog, k6.

Row 4: K6, yo, p2tog, k10, yo, p2tog, k3.

Row 5: K3, yo, p2tog, k3, yo, k2tog, k2, yo, k2tog, k1, yo, p2tog, k6.

Row 6: K6, yo, p2tog, k10, yo, p2tog, k3.

Row 7: K3, yo, p2tog, k4, yo, k2tog, k2, yo, k2tog, yo, p2tog, k6.

Row 8: BO 3, k2, yo, p2tog, k10, yo, p2tog, k3—20 sts.

Repeat Rows 1–8 for desired length. BO on Row 8.

Heart Lace #2

CO 15 sts.

Set-up row: Knit.

Row 1: K2, yo, p2tog, k2, yo twice, k2tog, [yo, k1] 2 times, yo twice, k2tog, k1, yo twice, k2—21 sts.

Row 2: K3, p1, k3, p6, k1, p1, k2, yo, p2tog, k2.

Row 3: K2, yo, p2tog, k2, yo twice, k2tog, k2, yo, k1, yo, k3, yo twice, k2tog, k5—25 sts.

Row 4: BO 2, k4, p10, k1, p1, k2, yo, p2tog, k2—23 sts.

Row 5: K2, yo, p2tog, k2, yo twice, k2tog, k4, yo, k1, yo, k5, yo twice, k2tog, k1, yo twice, k2—29 sts.

Row 6: K3, p1, k3, p14, k1, p1, k2, yo, p2tog, k2.

Row 7: K2, yo, p2tog, k1, k2tog, yo twice, k3tog, k9, k3tog, yo twice, k2tog, k5—27 sts.

Row 8: BO 2, k4, p12, k1, p1, k2, yo, p2tog, k2—25 sts.

Row 9: K2, yo, p2tog, k1, k2tog, yo twice, k3tog, k7, k3tog, yo twice, k2tog, k1, yo twice, k2.

Row 10: K3, p1, k3, p10, k1, p1, k2, yo, p2tog, k2.

Row 11: K2, yo, p2tog, k1, k2tog, yo twice, k3tog, k5, k3tog, yo twice, k2tog, k5—23 sts.

Row 12: BO 2, k4, p8, k1, p1, k2, yo, p2tog, k2—21 sts.

Row 13: K2, yo, p2tog, k1, k2tog, yo twice, k3tog, k3, k3tog, yo twice, k2tog, k1, yo twice, k2.

Row 14: K3, p1, k3, p6, k1, p1, k2, yo, p2tog, k2.

Row 15: K2, yo, p2tog, k1, k2tog, yo twice, k3tog, k4tog, pass first dec over second dec, yo twice, k2tog, k5—17 sts.

Row 16: BO 2, k4, p2, k1, p1, k2, yo, p2tog, k2—15 sts.

Repeat Rows 1–16 for desired length. BO on Row 16.

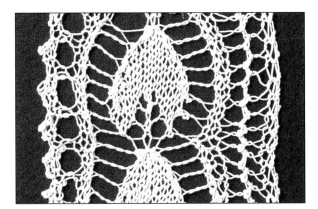

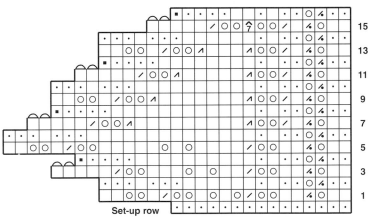

Mrs. R's Diamond Lace

CO 27 sts.

Set-up row: Knit.

Row 1: Sl 1, k2, [yo, k2tog] 2 times, k7, [k2tog, yo] 2 times, k3, yo, k2tog, yo, k2, yo, p2tog—28 sts.

Row 2 and all even-numbered rows: YO, p2tog, knit to end.

Row 3: Sl 1, k2, [yo, k2tog] 2 times, k6, [k2tog, yo] 2 times, k5, yo, k2tog, yo, k2, yo, p2tog—29 sts.

Row 5: Sl 1, k2, [yo, k2tog] 2 times, k5, [k2tog, yo] 2 times, k7, yo, k2tog, yo, k2, yo, p2tog—30 sts.

Row 7: Sl 1, k2, [yo, k2tog] 2 times, k4, [k2tog, yo] 2 times, k4, yo, k2tog, k3, yo, k2tog, yo, k2, yo, p2tog—31 sts.

Row 9: Sl 1, k2, [yo, k2tog] 2 times, k3, [k2tog, yo] 2 times, k4, [yo, k2tog] 2 times, k3, yo, k2tog, yo, k2, yo, p2tog—32 sts.

Row 11: Sl 1, k2, [yo, k2tog] 2 times, k2, [k2tog, yo] 2 times, k4, [yo, k2tog] 3 times, k3, yo, k2tog, yo, k2, yo, p2tog—33 sts.

Row 13: Sl 1, k2, [yo, k2tog] 2 times, k1, [k2tog, yo] 2 times, k4, [yo, k2tog] 4 times, k3, yo, k2tog, yo, k2, yo, p2tog—34 sts.

Row 15: Sl 1, k2, [yo, k2tog] 2 times, k3, [yo, k2tog] 2 times, k3, [yo, k2tog] 3 times, k2, k2tog, [yo, k2tog] 2 times, k1, yo, p2tog—33 sts.

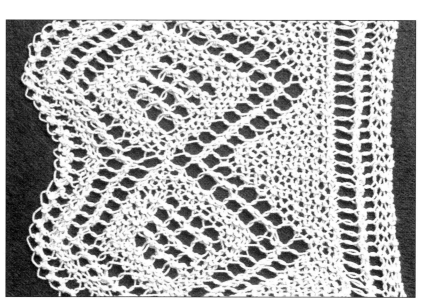

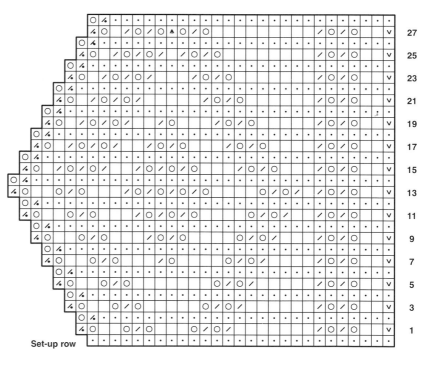

Set-up row

Row 17: Sl 1, k2, [yo, k2tog] 2 times, k4, [yo, k2tog] 2 times, k3, [yo, k2tog] 2 times, k2, k2tog, [yo, k2tog] 2 times, k1, yo, p2tog—32 sts.

Row 19: Sl 1, k2, [yo, k2tog] 2 times, k5, [yo, k2tog] 2 times, k3, yo, k2tog, k2, k2tog, [yo, k2tog] 2 times, k1, yo, p2tog—31 sts.

Row 21: Sl 1, k2, [yo, k2tog] 2 times, k6, [yo, k2tog] 2 times, k5, k2tog, [yo, k2tog] 2 times, k1, yo, p2tog—30 sts.

Row 23: Sl 1, k2, [yo, k2tog] 2 times, k7, [yo, k2tog] 2 times, k3, k2tog, [yo, k2tog] 2 times, k1, yo, p2tog—29 sts.

Row 25: Sl 1, k2, [yo, k2tog] 2 times, k8, [yo, k2tog] 2 times, k1, k2tog, [yo, k2tog] 2 times, k1, yo, p2tog—28 sts.

Row 27: Sl 1, k2, [yo, k2tog] 2 times, k9, yo, k2tog, yo, sl 1, k2tog, psso, [yo, k2tog] 2 times, k1, yo, p2tog—27 sts.

Repeat Rows 1–28 for desired length. BO on Row 28.

Knitted Pointed Edging #1

CO 16 sts.

Set-up row: Knit.

Row 1: [K2, yo, p2tog] 2 times, k1, [yo, k2tog] 3 times, yo, k1—17 sts.

Row 2 and all even-numbered rows through 18: Knit to last 8 sts, [yo, p2tog, k2] 2 times.

Row 3: [K2, yo, p2tog] 2 times, k2, [yo, k2tog] 3 times, yo, k1—18 sts.

Row 5: [K2, yo, p2tog] 2 times, k3, [yo, k2tog] 3 times, yo, k1—19 sts.

Row 7: [K2, yo, p2tog] 2 times, k4, [yo, k2tog] 3 times, yo, k1—20 sts.

Row 9: [K2, yo, p2tog] 2 times, k5, [yo, k2tog] 3 times, yo, k1—21 sts.

Row 11: [K2, yo, p2tog] 2 times, k6, [yo, k2tog] 3 times, yo, k1—22 sts.

Row 13: [K2, yo, p2tog] 2 times, k7, [yo, k2tog] 3 times, yo, k1—23 sts.

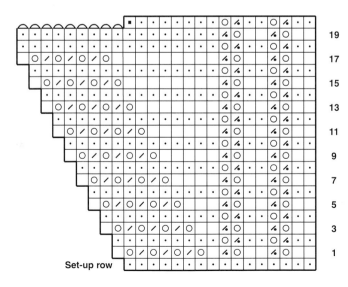

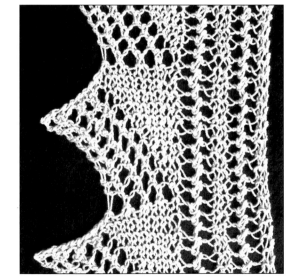

Row 15: [K2, yo, p2tog] 2 times, k8, [yo, k2tog] 3 times, yo, k1—24 sts.

Row 17: [K2, yo, p2tog] 2 times, k9, [yo, k2tog] 3 times, yo, k1—25 sts.

Row 19: [K2, yo, p2tog] 2 times, knit to end.

Row 20: BO 9, knit to last 8 sts, [yo, p2tog, k2] 2 times—16 sts.

Repeat Rows 1–20 for desired length. BO on Row 20.

Vine Lace

CO 32 sts.

Set-up row: Purl.

Row 1: YO, k1, yo, k2, k2tog twice, k2, yo, k2tog twice, yo, k2tog, yo, k1, yo, k2, k2tog, k4, k2tog, k2, yo, k2tog, yo, k2.

Row 2 and all even-numbered rows: Purl.

Row 3: YO, k3, yo, k1, k2tog twice, [k1, yo, k2tog] 2 times, yo, k3, yo, k2, [k2tog, k2] 2 times, [yo, k2tog] 2 times, k1.

Row 5: YO, k5, yo, k2tog twice, yo, k2tog, k1, yo, k2tog, yo, k5, yo, k2, k2tog twice, k2, [yo, k2tog] 2 times, k1.

Row 7: YO, k3, k2tog, k2, [yo, k2tog] 2 times, [k2tog, yo] 2 times, k2, k2tog, k4, k2tog, k2, yo, k1, yo, k2tog, yo, k2.

Row 9: YO, k1, yo, k2, k2tog twice, k2, yo, k2tog twice, yo, k2tog, yo, k2, k2tog, k2, k2tog, k2, yo, k3, yo, k2tog, yo, k2.

Row 11: YO, k3, yo, k1, k2tog twice, k1, yo, k2tog twice, yo, k2tog, yo, k2, k2tog twice, k2, yo, k5, yo, k2tog, yo, k2.

Row 13: YO, k5, yo, k2tog twice, yo, k2tog, k1, yo, k2tog, yo, k1, yo, k2, k2tog, k4, k2tog, k2, [yo, k2tog] 2 times, k1.

Row 15: YO, k3, k2tog, k2, [yo, k2tog] 2 times, k1, yo, k2tog, yo, k3, yo, k2, [k2tog, k2] 2 times, [yo, k2tog] 2 times, k1.

Row 17: YO, k1, yo, k2, k2tog twice, k2, yo, k2tog, k1, yo, k2tog, yo, k5, yo, k2, k2tog twice, k2, [yo, k2tog] 2 times, k1.

Row 19: YO, k3, yo, k1, k2tog twice, k1, yo, k2tog twice, yo, k2tog, yo, k2, k2tog, k4, k2tog, k2, yo, k1, yo, k2tog, yo, k2.

Row 21: YO, k5, [yo, k2tog twice] 2 times, yo, k2tog, yo, k2, [k2tog, k2] 2 times, yo, k3, yo, k2tog, yo, k2.

Row 23: YO, k3, k2tog, k2, [yo, k2tog] 2 times, [k2tog, yo] 2 times, k2, k2tog twice, k2, yo, k5, yo, k2tog, yo, k2.

Repeat Rows 1–24 for desired length. BO on Row 24.

Set-up row

Purl all even-numbered rows.

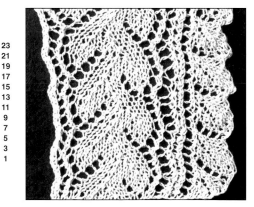

Knitted Lace #2

CO 13 sts.

Set-up row: Knit.

Row 1: Sl 1, k2, yo, k2tog, k1, [yo twice, k2tog] 3 times, k1—16 sts.

Row 2: K3, p1, [k2, p1] 2 times, k2, yo, k2tog, k2.

Rows 3, 7, and 11: Sl 1, k2, yo, k2tog, knit to end.

Row 4: K12, yo, k2tog, k2.

Row 5: Sl 1, k2, yo, k2tog, k1, yo twice, k2tog, knit to end—17 sts.

Row 6: K10, p1, k2, yo, k2tog, k2.

Row 8: K13, yo, k2tog, k2.

Row 9: Sl 1, k2, yo, k2tog, k1, [yo twice, k2tog] 2 times, k2, k2tog, yo twice, k2tog, k1—19 sts.

Row 10: K3, p1, k5, [p1, k2] 2 times, yo, k2tog, k2.

Row 12: BO 6, k8, yo, k2tog, k2— 13 sts.

Repeat Rows 1–12 for desired length. BO on Row 12.

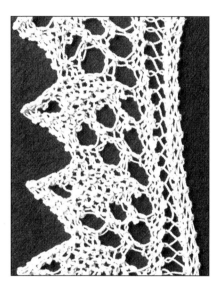

Set-up row

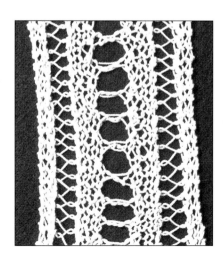

Insertion to Match Lace

CO 16 sts.

Set-up row: Knit.

Row 1: Sl 1, k2, yo, k2tog, k1, k2tog, yo twice, k2tog, k2, yo, k2tog, k2.

Row 2: Sl 1, k2, yo, k2tog, k3, p1, k3, yo, k2tog, k2.

Rows 3 and 4: Sl 1, k2, yo, k2tog, k7, yo, k2tog, k2.

Repeat Rows 1–4 for desired length. BO in knit after Row 4.

Set-up row

Shell and Shamrock Lace

CO 23 sts.

Set-up row: Knit.

Row 1: Sl 1, k1, yo, p2tog, k2tog, yo twice, k2tog, k4, [yo, k2tog] 2 times, [yo] 3 times, k2tog, k3, yo, p2tog—25 sts.

Row 2: YO, p2tog, k4, p1, k1, p1, k10, p1, k1, yo, p2tog, k2.

Row 3: Sl 1, k1, yo, p2tog, k2, k2tog, yo twice, k2tog, k3, [yo, k2tog] 2 times, k4, [yo] 4 times, k2tog, yo, p2tog—28 sts.

Row 4: YO, p2tog, k2, p1, k1, p1, k13, p1, k3, yo, p2tog, k2.

Row 5: Sl 1, k1, yo, p2tog, k2tog, yo twice, k2tog twice, yo twice, k2tog, k2, [yo, k2tog] 2 times, k2, [yo] 4 times, k2tog, k4, yo, p2tog—31 sts.

Row 6: YO, p2tog, k1, [yo, k2tog] 2 times, [k1, p1] 2 times, k10, p1, k3, p1, k1, yo, p2tog, k2.

Row 7: Sl 1, k1, yo, p2tog, k2, k2tog, yo twice, k2tog twice, yo twice, k2tog, k1, [yo, k2tog] 2 times, k10, yo, p2tog.

Row 8: YO, p2tog, k1, [yo, k2tog] 2 times, k12, [p1, k3] 2 times, yo, p2tog, k2.

Row 9: Sl 1, k1, yo, p2tog, k2tog, yo twice, k2tog twice, yo twice, k2tog, k4, [yo, k2tog] 2 times, k9, yo, p2tog.

Row 10: YO, p2tog, k3, [yo, k2tog] 2 times, k12, p1, k3, p1, k1, yo, p2tog, k2.

Row 11: Sl 1, k1, yo, p2tog, k2, k2tog, yo twice, k2tog, k7, [yo, k2tog] 2 times, k8, yo, p2tog.

Row 12: YO, p2tog, k4, [yo, k2tog] 2 times, k13, p1, k3, yo, p2tog, k2.

Row 13: Sl 1, k1, yo, p2tog, k2tog, yo twice, k2tog, k10, [yo, k2tog] 2 times, k7, yo, p2tog.

Row 14: YO, p2tog, k5, [yo, k2tog] 2 times, k14, p1, k1, yo, p2tog, k2.

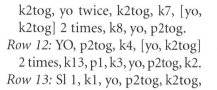

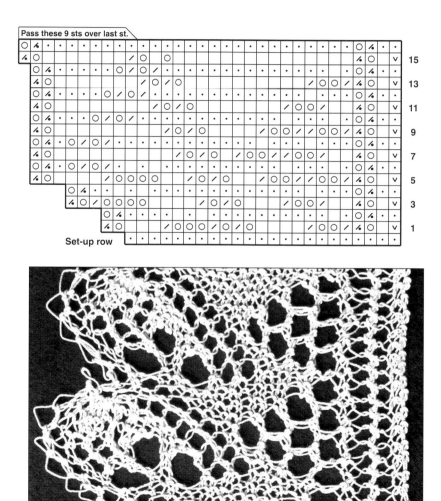

Row 15: Sl 1, k1, yo, p2tog, k15, yo, k1, yo, k2tog, k7, yo, p2tog—32 sts.

Row 16: YO, p2tog, k8, pass first 9 sts over last st on right needle, k18, yo, p2tog, k2—23 sts.

Repeat Rows 1–16 for desired length. BO on Row 16 after passing 9 sts over.

Sawtooth Edging

CO 13 sts.

Set-up row: Knit.

Row 1: K2, k2tog, yo twice, k2tog, k1, yo, k1, k2tog, yo, k2tog, k1.

Row 2 and all even-numbered rows through 16: Knit, working k1, p1 into each "yo twice".

Row 3: K2, k2tog, yo twice, k2tog, k1, yo, k1, k2tog, yo twice, k2tog, k1—14 sts.

Row 5: K2, k2tog, yo twice, k2tog, k1, yo, k2, k2tog, yo twice, k2tog, k1—15 sts.

Row 7: K2, k2tog, yo twice, k2tog, k1, yo, k3, k2tog, yo twice, k2tog, k1—16 sts.

Row 9: K2, k2tog, yo twice, k2tog, k1, yo, k4, k2tog, yo twice, k2tog, k1—17 sts.

Row 11: K2, k2tog, yo twice, k2tog, k1, yo, k5, k2tog, yo twice, k2tog, k1—18 sts.

Row 13: K2, k2tog, yo twice, k2tog, k1, yo, k6, k2tog, yo twice, k2tog, k1—19 sts.

Row 15: K2, k2tog, yo twice, k2tog, k1, yo, k7, k2tog, yo twice, k2tog, k1—20 sts.

Row 17: K2, k2tog, yo twice, k2tog, k1, yo, k13.

Row 18: BO 8, k8, p1, k3—13sts.

Repeat Rows 1–18 for desired length. BO on Row 18.

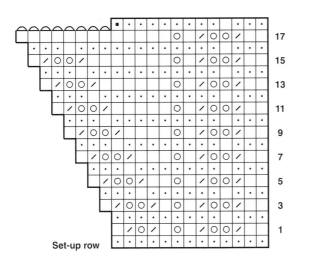

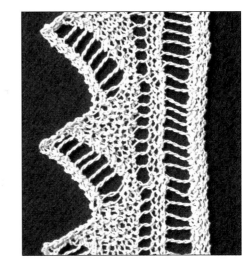

Rose Point Lace

CO 15 sts.

Set-up row: Knit.

Row 1: Sl 1, k2, yo, k2tog, k7, yo, k3—16 sts.

Rows 2, 4 and 6: Knit.

Row 3: Sl 1, k2, yo, k2tog, k8, yo, k3—17 sts.

Row 5: Sl 1, k2, yo, k2tog, k9, yo, k3—18 sts.

Row 7: Sl 1, k2, yo, k2tog, k3, k2tog, yo twice, k2tog, k3, yo, k3—19 sts.

Row 8: K9, p1, k9.

Row 9: Sl 1, k2, yo, k2tog, k1, k2tog, yo twice, k2tog twice, yo twice, k2tog, k2, yo, k3—20 sts.

Row 10: K8, p1, k3, p1, k7.

Row 11: Sl 1, k2, yo, k2tog, k3, k2tog, yo twice, k2tog, k5, yo, k3—21 sts.

Row 12: K11, p1, k9.

Row 13: Sl 1, k2, yo, k2tog, k1, k2tog, yo twice, k2tog twice, yo twice, k2tog, k3, yo, k2tog, k2.

Row 14: K4, k2tog, [k3, p1] 2 times, k7—20 sts.

Row 15: Sl 1, k2, yo, k2tog, k3, k2tog, yo twice, k2tog, k4, yo, k2tog, k2.

Row 16: K4, k2tog, k4, p1, k9—19 sts.

Row 17: Sl 1, k2, yo, k2tog, k10, yo, k2tog, k2.

Row 18: K4, k2tog, k13—18 sts.

Row 19: Sl 1, k2, yo, k2tog, k9, yo, k2tog, k2.

Row 20: K4, k2tog, k12—17 sts.

Row 21: Sl 1, k2, yo, k2tog, k8, yo, k2tog, k2.

Row 22: K4, k2tog, k11—16 sts.

Row 23: Sl 1, k2, yo, k2tog, k7, yo, k2tog, k2.

Row 24: K4, k2tog, k10.

Repeat Rows 1–24 for desired length. BO in knit after Row 24.

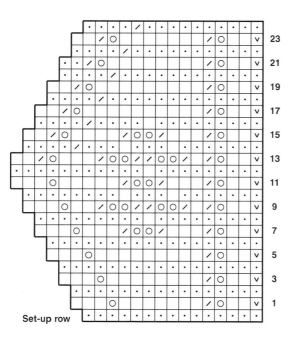

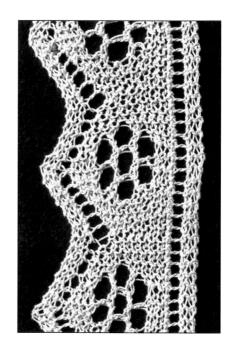

German Lace

CO 31 sts.

Set-up row: Knit.

Row 1: YO, k2tog, k1, yo, k3, [yo, k2tog, k1] 2 times, k2tog, yo, k1, k2tog, yo, k3, yo, k2tog, k4, k2tog, yo, k3—32 sts.

Row 2 and all even-numbered rows: Knit.

Row 3: YO, k2tog, k1, yo, k5, yo, k2tog, k1, yo, sl 1, k2tog, psso, yo, k1, k2tog, yo, k5, yo, k2tog, k3, k2tog, yo, k3—33 sts.

Row 5: YO, k2tog, k1, yo, k1, k2tog, yo, [k1, yo, k2tog] 2 times, k3, [k2tog, yo, k1] 2 times, yo, k2tog, k1, yo, k2tog, k2, k2tog, yo, k3—34 sts.

Row 7: YO, k2tog, k1, yo, k1, k2tog, yo, k3, [yo, k2tog, k1] 2 times, k2tog, yo, k1, k2tog, yo, k3, [yo, k2tog, k1] 2 times, k2tog, yo, k3—35 sts.

Row 9: YO, k2tog, k1, yo, k1, k2tog, yo, k5, yo, k2tog, k1, yo, sl 1, k2tog, psso, yo, k1, k2tog, yo, k5, yo, k2tog, k1, yo, k2tog twice, yo, k3—36 sts.

Row 11: YO, k2tog, k1, yo, k2tog twice, yo, k4, k2tog, yo, k2tog, [k1, yo] 2 times, k2tog twice, yo, k4, k2tog, yo, k2tog, k1, yo, k1, k2tog, yo, k3.

Row 13: YO, k2tog twice, [yo, k2tog, k1] 2 times, k2tog, yo, k1, k2tog, yo, k3, [yo, k2tog, k1] 2 times, k2tog, yo, k1, k2tog, yo, k2, k2tog, yo, k3—35 sts.

Row 15: YO, k2tog twice, yo, k2tog, k1, yo, sl 1, k2tog, psso, yo, k1, k2tog, yo, k5, yo, k2tog, k1, yo, sl 1, k2tog, psso, yo, k1, k2tog, yo, k3, k2tog, yo, k3—34 sts.

Row 17: YO, k2tog twice, yo, k2tog, k3, [k2tog, yo, k1] 2 times, yo, k2tog, k1, yo, k2tog, k3, k2tog, yo, k4, k2tog, yo, k3—33 sts.

Row 19: YO, k2tog twice, yo, k2tog, k1, k2tog, yo, k1, k2tog, yo, k3, [yo, k2tog, k1] 2 times, k2tog, yo, k5, k2tog, yo, k3—32 sts.

Row 21: YO, k2tog twice, yo, sl 1, k2tog, psso, yo, k1, k2tog, yo, k5, yo, k2tog, k1, yo, sl 1, k2tog, psso, yo, k6, k2tog, yo, k3—31 sts.

Row 23: YO, k2tog twice, yo, k1, yo, k2tog twice, yo, k4, [k2tog, yo, k1] 2 times, yo, k2tog, k5, k2tog, yo, k3—31 sts.

Repeat Rows 1–24 for desired length. BO on Row 24.

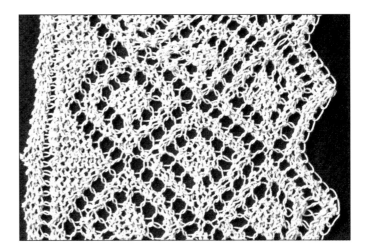

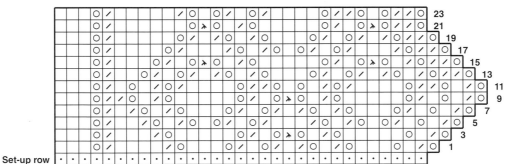

Set-up row

Knit all even-numbered rows.

Double Rose Leaf Lace

CO 27 sts.

Set-up row: Knit.

Row 1: Sl 1, k2, yo, k2tog, k1, yo, k1, ssk, p1, k2tog, k1, p1, k1, ssk, p1, k2tog, k1, yo, k2, yo, k2tog, yo twice, k2.

Row 2: K3, p1, k1, yo, k2tog, p4, k1, [p2, k1] 2 times, p4, k1, yo, k2tog, k2.

Row 3: Sl 1, k2, yo, k2tog, k1, yo, k1, yo, ssk, p1, k2tog, p1, ssk, p1, k2tog, yo, k1, yo, k2, yo, k2tog, k4.

Row 4: K5, yo, k2tog, p5, [k1, p1] 2 times, k1, p5, k1, yo, k2tog, k2.

Row 5: Sl 1, k2, yo, k2tog, k1, yo, k3, yo, sl 1, k2tog, psso, p1, sl 1, k2tog, psso, yo, k3, yo, k2, yo, [k2tog, yo twice] 2 times, k2—30 sts.

Row 6: K3, p1, k2, p1, k1, yo, k2tog, [p7, k1] 2 times, yo, k2tog, k2.

Row 7: Sl 1, k2, yo, k2tog, k1, yo, k5, yo, sl 1, k2tog, psso, yo, k5, yo, k2, yo, k2tog, k7—32 sts.

Row 8: BO 5, k2, yo, k2tog, p17, k1, yo, k2tog, k2.

Repeat Rows 1–8 for desired length. BO in knit after Row 8.

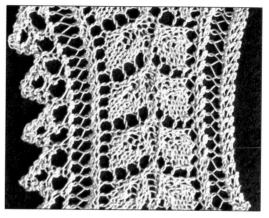

Leaf Point Apron Lace

CO 31 sts.

Set-up row: Knit.

Row 1: Sl 1, k2, yo, k2tog, [k1, yo, k1, k2tog, k1 tbl, k2tog, k1, yo] 2 times, k2, yo, k2tog, k1, yo twice, k2tog, k1, yo, k2tog—32 sts.

Row 2: K5, p1, k5, p7, k1, p7, k6.

Row 3: Sl 1, k2, yo, k2tog, k1, yo, k1, k2tog, k1 tbl, k2tog, k1, p1, k1, k2tog, k1 tbl, k2tog, k1, yo, k2, yo, k2tog, k7—30 sts.

Row 4: K11, p6, k1, p6, k6.

Row 5: Sl 1, k2, yo, k2tog, [k1, yo] 2 times, k2tog, k1 tbl, k2tog, p1, k2tog, k1 tbl, k2tog, yo, k1, yo, k2, yo, k2tog, k1, [yo twice, k2tog] 2 times, yo, k2tog—32 sts.

Row 6: K4, p1, k2, p1, k5, p6, k1, p6, k6.

Row 7: Sl 1, k2, yo, k2tog, k1, yo, k3, yo, k3tog, p1, k3tog, yo, k3, yo, k2, yo, k2tog, k9.

Row 8: K13, p6, k1, p6, k6.

Row 9: Sl 1, k2, yo, k2tog, k1, yo, k5, yo, k3tog, yo, k5, yo, k2, yo, k2tog, k1, [yo twice, k2tog] 3 times, yo, k2tog—37 sts.

Row 10: K4, [p1, k2] 2 times, p1, k5, p7, k1, p7, k6.

Row 11: Sl 1, k2, yo, k2tog, [k1, yo, k1, k2tog, k1 tbl, k2tog, k1, yo] 2 times, k2, yo, k2tog, k12.

Row 12: K16, p7, k1, p7, k6.

Row 13: Sl 1, k2, yo, k2tog, k1, yo,

k1, k2tog, k1 tbl, k2tog, k1, p1, k1, k2tog, k1 tbl, k2tog, k1, yo, k2, yo, k2tog, k1, yo twice, k3 tog, [yo twice, k2tog] 3 times, yo, k2tog—38 sts.

Row 14: K4, [p1, k2] 3 times, p1, k5, p6, k1, p6, k6.

Row 15: Sl 1, k2, yo, k2tog, [k1, yo] 2 times, k2tog, k1 tbl, k2tog, p1, k2tog, k1 tbl, k2tog, yo, k1, yo, k2, yo, k2tog, k15.

Rows 16 and 18: K19, p6, k1, p6, k6.

Row 17: Sl 1, k2, yo, k2tog, k1, yo, k3, yo, k3tog, p1, k3tog, yo, k3, yo, k2, yo, k2tog, k1, [yo, k2tog] 7 times.

Row 19: Sl 1, k2, yo, k2tog, k1, yo, k5, yo, k3tog, yo, k5, yo, k2, yo, k2tog, k15—40 sts.

Row 20: BO 9 sts, k9, p7, k1, p7, k6—31 sts.

Repeat Rows 1–20 for desired length. BO on Row 20.

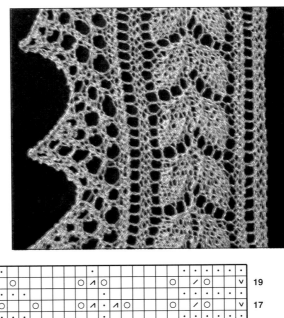

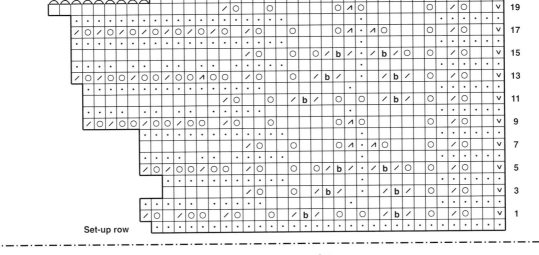

Fern Leaf Lace

CO 35 sts.

Set-up row: Knit.

Row 1: K3, [yo, k2tog] 2 times, k2tog, k5, [yo, k1] 3 times, yo, k5, k2tog, k1, [yo, k2tog] 2 times, [yo twice, k2tog, k1] 2 times—39 sts.

Row 2: [K3, p1] 2 times, k1, [yo, k2tog] 2 times, p2tog, p15, p2tog, k1, [yo, k2tog] 2 times, k2—37 sts.

Row 3: K3, [yo, k2tog] 2 times, k2tog, k4, yo, k1, yo, k3, yo, k1, yo, k4, k2tog, k1, [yo, k2tog] 2 times, yo twice, k2tog, k6—40 sts.

Row 4: K2, [yo twice, k2tog] 2 times, k2, p1, k1, [yo, k2tog] 2 times, p2tog, p15, p2tog, k1, [yo, k2tog] 2 times, k2.

Row 5: K3, [yo, k2tog] 2 times, k2tog, k3, yo, k1, yo, k5, yo, k1, yo, k3, k2tog, k1, [yo, k2tog] 2 times, yo twice, k2tog, k3, [p1, k2] 2 times—43 sts.

Row 6: K11, p1, k1, [yo, k2tog] 2 times, p2tog, p15, p2tog, k1, [yo, k2tog] 2 times, k2—41 sts.

Row 7: K3, [yo, k2tog] 2 times, k2tog, k2, yo, k1, yo, k7, yo, k1, yo, k2, k2tog, k1, [yo, k2tog] 2 times, yo twice, k2tog, k1, [yo twice, k2tog] 4 times, k1—48 sts.

Row 8: K3, [p1, k2], 3 times, p1, k3, p1, k1, [yo, k2tog] 2 times, p2tog, p15, p2tog, k1, [yo, k2tog] 2 times, k2—46 sts.

Row 9: K3, [yo, k2tog] 2 times, k2tog, [k1, yo] 2 times, k9, [yo, k1] 2 times, k2tog, k1, [yo, k2tog] 2 times, yo twice, k2tog, k15—49 sts.

Row 10: BO 12, k4, p1, k1, [yo, k2tog] 2 times, p2tog, p15, p2tog, k1, [yo, k2tog] 2 times, k2—35 sts.

Repeat Rows 1–10 for desired length. BO in knit after Row 10.

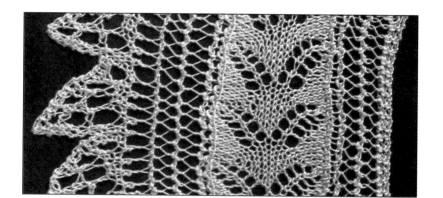

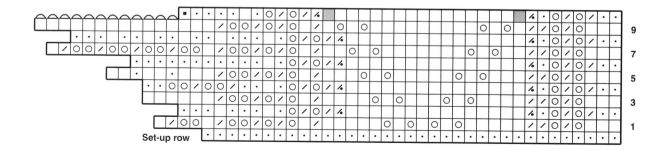

51

Mable Casis's Lace

CO 31 sts.

Set-up row: Knit.

Row 1: K8, k2tog, yo, k3, yo, k2tog, k9, k2tog, yo, k3, p1, yo, k1—32 sts.

Row 2: K2, yo, k5, yo, k2tog, k7, k2tog, yo, k5, yo, k2tog, k7—33 sts.

Row 3: K6, k2tog, yo, k7, yo, k2tog, k5, [k2tog, yo, k1] 2 times, yo, k2tog, k1, p1, yo, k1—34 sts.

Row 4: K2, yo, k1, k2tog, yo, k3, yo, k2tog, k1, yo, k2tog, k3, k2tog, yo, k9, yo, k2tog, k5—35 sts.

Row 5: K4, k2tog, yo, k11, yo, k2tog, k1, k2tog, yo, k1, k2tog, yo, k5, yo, k2tog, k1, p1, yo, k1—36 sts.

Row 6: K2, yo, k1, k2tog, yo, k3, yo, k2tog, k2, yo, k2tog, k1, yo, k3tog, yo, k13, yo, k2tog, k3—37 sts.

Row 7: K5, yo, k2tog, k9, k2tog, yo, k3, yo, k2tog, k1, yo, k2tog, k3, [k2tog, yo, k1] 2 times, k2tog—36 sts.

Row 8: BO 1, [k1, yo, k2tog] 2 times, [k1, k2tog, yo] 2 times, k5, yo, k2tog, k7, k2tog, yo, k6—35 sts.

Row 9: K7, yo, k2tog, k5, k2tog, yo, k7, yo, k2tog, k1, yo, sl 1, k2tog, psso, [yo, k1, k2tog] 2 times—34 sts.

Row 10: BO 1, k1, yo, k2tog, k3, k2tog, yo, k9, yo, k2tog, k3, k2tog, yo, k8—33 sts.

Row 11: K9, yo, k2tog, k1, k2tog, yo, k11, yo, k2tog, k1, k2tog, yo, k1, k2tog—32 sts.

Row 12: BO 1, k1, yo, k3tog, yo, k13, yo, k3tog, yo, k10—31 sts.

Repeat Rows 1–12 for desired length. BO in knit after Row 12.

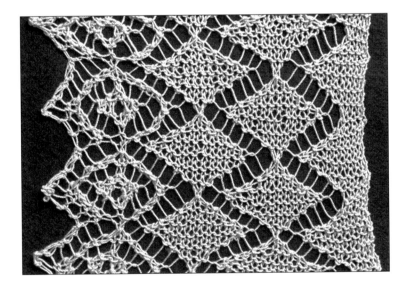

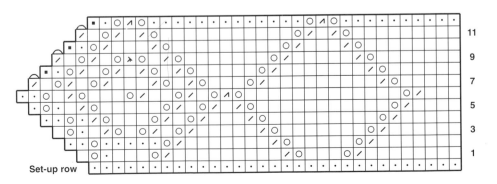

Set-up row

Hamburg Lace

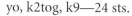

CO 22 sts.

Set-up row: Knit.

Row 1: Sl 1, k1, [yo, k2tog] 3 times, k4, k2tog, yo, k2, k2tog, yo, k1, yo, k3tog—21 sts.

Row 2: Sl l, yo, k3, yo, k2tog, k2, yo, k2tog, k11—22 sts.

Row 3: Sl 1, k9, k2tog, yo, k2, k2tog, yo, k5, yo, k1—23 sts.

Row 4: Sl 1, yo, k7, yo, k2tog, k2, yo, k2tog, k9—24 sts.

Row 5: Sl 1, k1, [yo, k2tog] 3 times, k2tog, yo, k2, k2tog, yo, k9, yo, k1—25 sts.

Row 6: K2, yo, k2tog, k5, k2tog, yo, k2, k2tog, yo, k10.

Row 7: Sl 1, k10, yo, k2tog, k2, yo, k2tog, k4, k2tog, yo, k2tog—24 sts.

Row 8: K2tog, yo, k2tog, [k2, k2tog, yo] 2 times, k12—23 sts.

Row 9: Sl 1, k1, [yo, k2tog] 3 times, k5, yo, k2tog, k2, [yo, k3tog] 2 times—21 sts.

Row 10: K2tog, yo, k1, yo, k2, k2tog, yo, k14—22 sts.

Row 11: Sl 1, k11, k2tog, yo, k2, k2tog, yo, k1, yo, k3tog—21 sts.

Repeat Rows 2–11 for desired length. BO on Row 11.

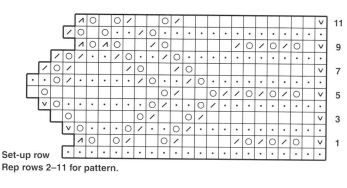

Set-up row
Rep rows 2–11 for pattern.

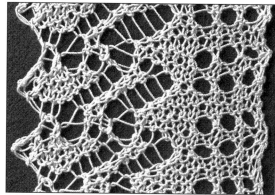

Daisy Lace

CO 26 sts.

Set-up row: Knit.

Row 1: Sl 1, k2, yo, p2tog, k5, k2tog, yo twice, k2tog, k3, [yo twice, k2tog] 2 times, yo, k2tog, k3—28 sts.

Row 2: K4, yo, k2tog, k1, p1, k2, p1, k5, p1, k6, yo, p2tog, k3.

Row 3: Sl 1, k2, yo, p2tog, k3, [k2tog, yo twice, k2tog] 2 times, k7, yo, k2tog, k3.

Row 4: K4, yo, k2tog, k8, p1, k3, p1, k4, yo, p2tog, k3.

Row 5: Sl 1, k2, yo, p2tog, k5, k2tog, yo twice, k2tog, k3, yo twice, k2tog, k4, yo, k2tog, k3—29 sts.

Row 6: K4, yo, k2tog, [k5, p1] 2 times, k6, yo, p2tog, k3.

Row 7: Sl 1, k2, yo, p2tog, k3, [k2tog, yo twice, k2tog] 2 times, k8, yo, k2tog, k3.

Row 8: BO 3, k3, yo, k2tog, k6, p1, k3, p1, k4, yo, p2tog, k3—26 sts.

Row 9: Sl 1, k2, yo, p2tog, k5, k2tog, yo twice, k2tog, k3, [yo twice, k2tog] 2 times, yo, k2tog, k3—28 sts.

Row 10: K4, yo, k2tog, k1, p1, k2, p1, k5, p1, k6, yo, p2tog, k3.

Row 11: Sl 1, k2, yo, p2tog, k18, yo, k2tog, k3.

Row 12: K4, yo, k2tog, k17, yo, p2tog, k3.

Row 13: Sl 1, k2, yo, p2tog, k12, yo twice, k2tog, k4, yo, k2tog, k3—29 sts.

Row 14: K4, yo, k2tog, k5, p1, k12, yo, p2tog, k3.

Row 15: Sl 1, k2, yo, p2tog, k19, yo, k2tog, k3.

Row 16: BO 3, k3, yo, k2tog, k15, yo, p2tog, k3—26 sts.

Repeat Rows 1–16 for desired length. BO on Row 16.

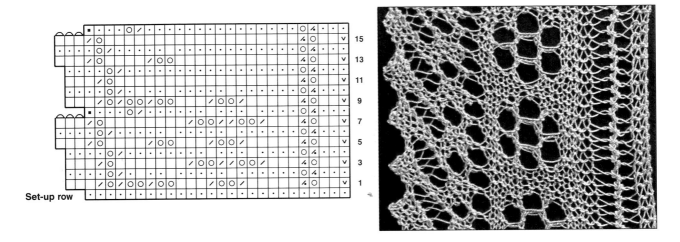

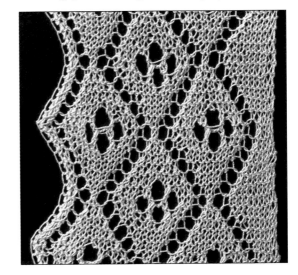

Dotted Diamond Lace

CO 32 sts.

Set-up row: Knit.

Row 1: Sl 1, k7, k2tog, yo, k3, yo, k2tog, k2, k2tog, yo twice, k2tog, k3, k2tog, [yo, k3] 2 times—33 sts.

Row 2: YO, k2tog, k12, p1, k18.

Row 3: Sl 1, k6, k2tog, yo, k5, yo, k2tog, k7, k2tog, yo, k5, yo, k3—34 sts.

Rows 4, 6, and 8: YO, k2tog, knit to end.

Row 5: Sl 1, k5, k2tog, yo, k7, yo, k2tog, k5, k2tog, yo, k7, yo, k3—35 sts.

Row 7: Sl 1, k4, k2tog, yo, k9, yo, k2tog, k3, k2tog, yo, k9, yo, k3—36 sts.

Row 9: Sl 1, k3, k2tog, yo, k3, k2tog, yo twice, k2tog, k4, yo, k2tog, k1, k2tog, yo, k3, k2tog, yo twice, k2tog, k4, yo, k3—37 sts.

Row 10: YO, k2tog, k8, p1, k15, p1, k10.

Row 11: Sl 1, k2, k2tog, yo, k2, [k2tog, yo twice, k2tog] 2 times, k3, yo, k3tog, yo, k2 [k2tog, yo twice, k2tog] 2 times, k3, yo, k3—38 sts.

Row 12: YO, k2tog, k7, p1, k3, p1, k11, p1, k3, p1, k8.

Row 13: Sl 1, k4, yo, k2tog, k2, k2tog, yo twice, k2tog, k3, k2tog, yo, k3, yo, k2tog, k2, k2tog, yo twice, k2tog, k3, k2tog, yo,

k2tog, k2—37 sts.

Row 14: YO, k2tog, k8, p1, k15, p1, k10.

Row 15: Sl 1, k5, yo, k2tog, k7, k2tog, yo, k5, yo, k2tog, k7, k2tog, yo, k2tog, k2—36 sts.

Rows 16, 18, and 20: YO, k2tog, knit to end.

Row 17: Sl 1, k6, yo, k2tog, k5, k2tog, yo, k7, yo, k2tog, k5, k2tog, yo, k2tog, k2—35 sts.

Row 19: Sl 1, k7, yo, k2tog, k3, k2tog, yo, k9, yo, k2tog, k3, k2tog, yo, k2tog, k2—34 sts.

Row 21: Sl 1, k8, yo, k2tog, k1, k2tog, yo, k3, k2tog, yo twice, k2tog, k4, yo, k2tog, k1, k2tog, yo, k2tog, k2—33 sts.

Row 22: YO, k2tog, k12, p1, k18.

Row 23: Sl 1, k9, yo, k3tog, yo, k2, [k2tog, yo twice, k2tog] 2 times, k3, yo, k3tog, yo, k2tog, k2—32 sts.

Row 24: YO, k2tog, k9, p1, k3, p1, k16.

Repeat Rows 1–24 for desired length. BO on Row 24.

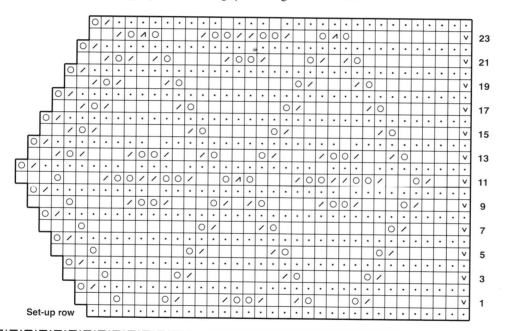

Combination Lace

CO 29 sts.

Set-up row: Knit.

Row 1: K3, yo, k2tog, k1, [yo, k2tog] 3 times, k5, yo, k2tog,

k3, yo, k1, yo, k6—31 sts.

Row 2: [K13, yo, k2tog] 2 times, k1.

Row 3: K3, yo, k2tog, k2, [yo,

k2tog] 3 times, k4, yo, k2tog, k1, k2tog, yo, k3, yo, k6—32 sts.

Row 4: K14, yo, k2tog, k13, yo, k2tog, k1.

Row 5: K3, yo, k2tog, k3, [yo, k2tog] 3 times, k3, yo, k2tog twice, yo, k5, yo, k6—33 sts.

Row 6: K15, yo, k2tog, k13, yo, k2tog, k1.

Row 7: K3, yo, k2tog, k4, [yo, k2tog] 3 times, k2, yo, k3tog, yo, k2tog, k3, k2tog, yo, k6—32 sts.

Row 8: BO 3, k10, yo, k2tog, k13, yo, k2tog, k1—29 sts.

Row 9: K3, yo, k2tog, k5, [yo, k2tog] 3 times, [k1, yo, k2tog] 2 times, k1, k2tog, yo, k4.

Rows 10 and 12: K11, yo, k2tog, k13, yo, k2tog, k1.

Row 11: K3, yo, k2tog, k6, [yo, k2tog] 4 times, k2, yo, sl 1, k2tog, psso, yo, k5.

Repeat Rows 1–12 for desired length. BO in knit after Row 12.

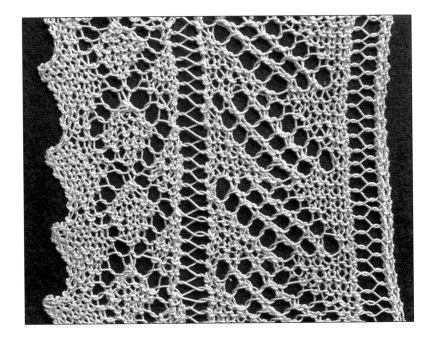

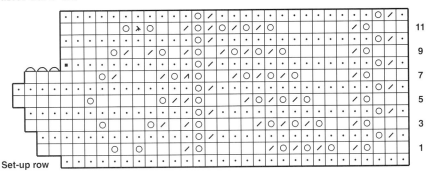

Scroll Leaf Lace

CO 23 sts.

Set-up row: Knit.

Row 1: Sl 1, k1, yo, ssk, k9, [yo, k2tog] 2 times, [yo] 4 times, k2tog, k1, yo, k2tog, k1—26 sts.

Row 2: K6, p1, k1, p1, k14, p1, k2.

Row 3: Sl 1, k1, yo, ssk, k3, k2tog, yo twice, k2tog, k3, [yo, k2tog] 2 times, k4, k2tog, yo, k2.

Rows 4, 8 and 12: K17, p1, k5, p1, k2.

Row 5: Sl 1, k1, yo, ssk, k1, [k2tog,

yo twice, k2tog] 2 times, k2, [yo, k2tog] 2 times, k3, k2tog, yo, k2.

Rows 6 and 10: K15, [p1, k3] 2 times, p1, k2.

Row 7: Sl 1, k1, yo, ssk, k3, k2tog, yo twice, k2tog, k5, [yo, k2tog]

2 times, k2, k2tog, yo, k2.

Row 9: Sl 1, k1, yo, ssk, k1, [k2tog, yo twice, k2tog] 2 times, k4, [yo, k2tog] 2 times, k1, k2tog, yo, k2.

Row 11: Sl 1, k1, yo, ssk, k3, k2tog, yo twice, k2tog, k7, [yo,

k2tog] 2 times, k2tog, yo, k2.

Row 13: Sl 1, k1, yo, ssk, k15, [yo, k2tog] 2 times, k3.

Row 14: BO 3, k19, p1, k2—23 sts. Repeat Rows 1–14 for desired length. BO on Row 14.

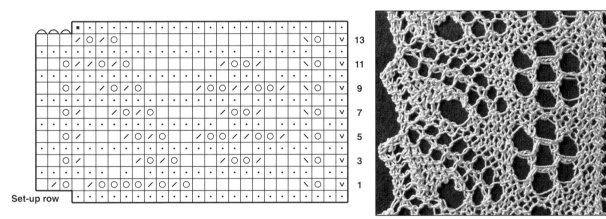

Delineator Leaf Lace

CO 25 sts.
Set-up row: Knit.

Row 1: [YO, k1, yo, k2, k2tog twice, k2] 2 times, [yo, k2tog] 3

times, k1—25 sts.
Rows 2, 4, 6, and 8: Purl.

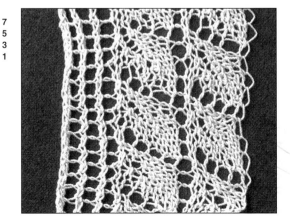

Purl all even-numbered rows.

Row 3: [YO, k3, yo, k1, k2tog twice, k1] 2 times, [yo, k2tog] 3 times, k1.

Row 5: [YO, k5, yo, k2tog twice] 2 times, [yo, k2tog] 3 times, k1.

Row 7: YO, k3, k2tog, k2, yo, k2tog, yo, k3, k2tog, k2, [yo, k2tog] 4 times, k1.

Repeat Rows 1–8 for desired length. BO on Row 8.

Knitted Lace #3

CO 16 sts.

Set-up row: Knit.

Row 1: Sl 1, k2, [yo twice, k2tog] 2 times, k6, yo twice, k2tog, k1— 19 sts.

Row 2: K3, p1, k8, p1, k2, p1, k3.

Rows 3, 7, and 11: Sl 1, knit to end.

Rows 4 and 8: Knit.

Row 5: Sl 1, k2, [yo twice, k2tog] 2 times, k7, [yo twice, k2tog] 2 times, k1—23 sts.

Row 6: K3, p1, k2, p1, k9, p1, k2, p1, k3.

Row 9: Sl 1, k2, [yo twice, k2tog] 2 times, [yo twice, sl 1, k2tog, psso] 5 times, k1—25 sts.

Row 10: K3, p1, [k2, p1] 6 times, k3.

Row 12: BO 9 sts, k15—16 sts.

Repeat Rows 1–12 for desired length. BO on Row 12.

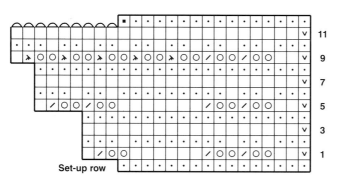

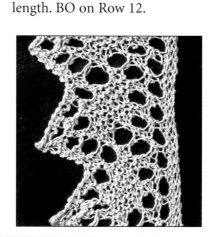

Novelty Lace

CO 37 sts.

Set-up row: Knit.

Row 1: K4, yo, p2tog, k1, [yo, k2tog, k1, k2tog, yo, k1] 3 times, yo, k2tog, k1, yo, p2tog, k1, yo, k2tog, [yo] 3 times, k2tog, yo, p2tog—39 sts.

Row 2: YO, p2tog, [k1, p1] 3 times, k1, yo, p2tog, p22, yo, p2tog, k4.

Row 3: K4, yo, p2tog, k1, [yo, k2tog, k1, k2tog, yo, k1] 3 times, yo, k2tog, k1, yo, p2tog, k2, yo, k5, yo, p2tog—40 sts.

Row 4: YO, p2tog, k5, p1, k2, yo, p2tog, p22, yo, p2tog, k4.

Row 5: K4, yo, p2tog, k1, [yo, k2tog, k1, k2tog, yo, k1] 3 times, yo, k2tog, k1, yo, p2tog, k3, yo, k2tog, k3, yo, p2tog.

Row 6: YO, p2tog, k4, p1, k3, yo, p2tog, p22, yo, p2tog, k4.

Row 7: K4, yo, p2tog, k2, [yo, k3tog, yo, k3] 3 times, yo, k2, yo, p2tog, k4, yo, k2tog, k2, yo, p2tog—41 sts.

Row 8: YO, p2tog, k3, p1, k4, yo, p2tog, p23, yo, p2tog, k4.

Row 9: K4, yo, p2tog, [k1, k2tog, yo, k1, yo, k2tog] 3 times, k1, k2tog, yo, k2, yo, p2tog, k5, yo, k2tog, k1, yo, p2tog.

Row 10: YO, p2tog, k2, p1, k5, yo, p2tog, p23, yo, p2tog, k4.

Row 11: K4, yo, p2tog, k2tog, [yo, k3, yo, k3tog] 3 times, yo, k2tog, k1, yo, p2tog, k6, yo, k2tog, yo, p2tog—40 sts.

Row 12: BO 3, place rem st onto left needle, yo, p2tog, k5, yo, p2tog, p22, yo, p2tog, k4—37 sts.

Repeat Rows 1–12 for desired length. BO on Row 12.

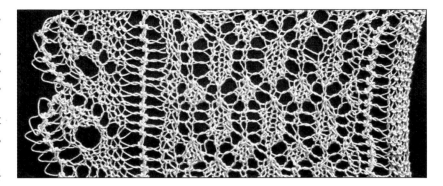

Set-up row

11

9

7

5

3

1

Wheel Lace

CO 31 sts.

Set-up row: Knit.

Row 1: K2, yo, k2tog, k1, yo, k2tog, k4, k2tog, yo twice, k2tog, k5, yo, k2tog, k1, [yo, k2tog] 3 times, yo, k2—32 sts.

Row 2: K11, yo, k2tog, k4, yo twice, k2tog twice, yo twice, k2tog, k9—33 sts.

Row 3: K2, yo, k2tog, k1, yo, k2tog, k4, p1, k3, p1, k5, yo, k2tog, k2, [yo, k2tog] 3 times, yo, k2—34 sts.

Row 4: K12, yo, k2tog, k5, k2tog, yo twice, k2tog, k11.

Row 5: K2, yo, k2tog, k1, yo, k2tog, k6, p1, k7, yo, k2tog, k3, [yo, k2tog] 3 times, yo, k2—35 sts.

Row 6: K13, yo, k2tog, k5, yo twice, k2tog twice, yo twice, k2tog, k9—36 sts.

Row 7: K2, yo, k2tog, k1, yo, k2tog, k4, p1, k3, p1, k6, yo, k2tog, k4, [yo, k2tog] 3 times, yo, k2—37 sts.

Row 8: K14, yo, k2tog, k6, k2tog, yo twice, k2tog, k11—37 sts.

Row 9: K2, yo, k2tog, k1, yo, k2tog, k6, drop extra yo, k2tog, k6, yo, k2tog, k5, [yo, k2tog] 3 times, yo, k2—36 sts.

Row 10: K15, yo, k2tog, k19.

Row 11: K2, yo, k2tog, k1, yo,

k2tog, k13, yo, k2tog, k14.

Row 12: BO 5, k9, yo, k2tog, k19—31 sts.

Repeat Rows 1–12 for desired length. BO on Row 12.

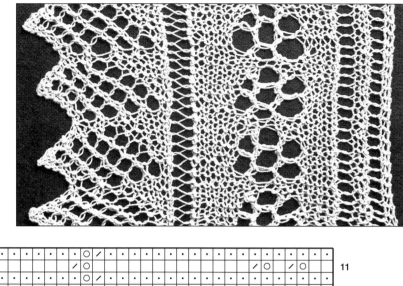

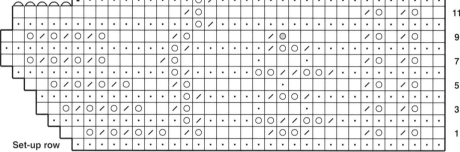

Shell Lace

CO 18 sts.

Set-up row: Knit.

Row 1: Sl 1, k1, [yo, ssk] 2 times, yo twice, k2tog, k7, yo twice, k2tog, k1—20 sts.

Row 2: YO twice, k2tog, k1, p1, k9, [p1, k1] 2 times, p1, k2—21 sts.

Row 3: Sl 1, k1, [yo, ssk] 2 times, k11, yo twice, k2tog, k1, drop extra yo.

Row 4: YO twice, k2tog, k1, p1, k12, p1, k1, p1, k2—22 sts.

Row 5: Sl 1, k1, [yo, ssk] 2 times, [yo twice, k2tog] 2 times, k8, yo twice, k2tog, k1, drop extra yo—24 sts.

Row 6: YO twice, k2tog, k1, p1, k10, p1, k2, [p1, k1] 2 times, p1, k2—25 sts.

Row 7: Sl 1, k1, [yo, ssk] 2 times, k15, yo twice, k2tog, k1, drop extra yo.

Row 8: YO twice, k2tog, k1, p1,

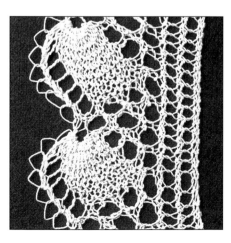

k16, p1, k1, p1, k2—26 sts.

Row 9: Sl 1, k1, [yo, ssk] 2 times, [yo twice, k2tog] 3 times, k10, yo twice, k2tog, k1, drop extra yo—29 sts.

Row 10: YO twice, k2tog, k1, p1, k12, [p1, k2] 2 times, [p1, k1] 2 times, p1, k2—30 sts.

Row 11: Sl 1, k1, [yo, ssk] 2 times,

k20, yo twice, k2tog, k1, drop extra yo.

Row 12: YO twice, k2tog, k1, p1, k21, p1, k1, p1, k2—31 sts.

Row 13: Sl 1, k1, [yo, ssk] 2 times, [yo twice, k2tog] 4 times, k13, yo twice, k2tog, k1, drop extra yo—35 sts.

Row 14: YO twice, k2tog, k1, p1,

k15, [p1, k2] 3 times, [p1, k1] 2 times, p1, k2—36 sts.

Row 15: Sl 1, k1, [yo, ssk] 2 times, k10, skip first st on left needle, pass next 16 sts over first st, k1, drop extra yo—18 sts.

Row 16: K13, p1, k1, p1, k2.

Repeat Rows 1–16 for desired length. BO on Row 16.

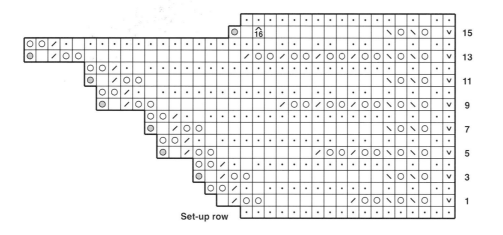

Knitted Oak Leaf Lace

CO 22 sts.

Set-up row: Knit.

Row 1: [K2, yo, p2tog] 4 times, k1, [yo twice, k2tog] 2 times, k1— 24 sts.

Row 2: K3, p1, k2, p1, k1, [yo, p2tog, k2] 4 times.

Row 3: [K2, yo, p2tog] 4 times, k3, [yo twice, k2tog] 2 times, k1— 26 sts.

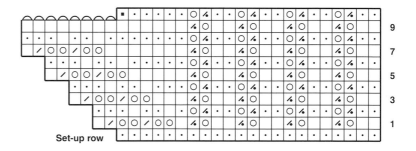

Row 4: K3, p1, k2, p1, k3, [yo, p2tog, k2] 4 times.

Row 5: [K2, yo, p2tog] 4 times, k5, [yo twice, k2tog] 2 times, k1—28 sts.

Row 6: K3, p1, k2, p1, k5, [yo, p2tog, k2] 4 times.

Row 7: [K2, yo, p2tog] 4 times, k7, [yo twice, k2tog] 2 times, k1—30 sts.

Row 8: K3, p1, k2, p1, k7, [yo, p2tog, k2] 4 times.

Row 9: [K2, yo, p2tog] 4 times, k14.

Row 10: BO 8 sts, k5, [yo, p2tog, k2] 4 times—22 sts.

Repeat Rows 1–10 for desired length. BO in knit after Row 10.

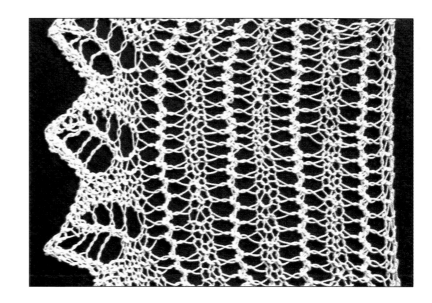

Altoona Lace

CO 23 sts.

Set-up row: Knit.

Row 1: K1, k2tog, yo twice, k2tog, k3, [k2tog, yo twice, k2tog] 2 times, k5, yo, k2—24 sts.

Rows 2, 4, 6, 10, 12, and 14: Knit, working (k1, p1) in each "yo twice".

Row 3: K10, k2tog, yo twice, k2tog, k8, yo, k2—25 sts.

Row 5: K1, k2tog, yo twice, k2tog,

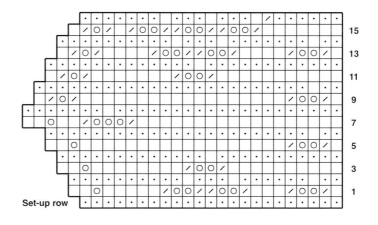

k18, yo, k2—26 sts.

Row 7: K18, k2tog, [yo] 3 times, k2tog, k2, yo, k2—28 sts.

Row 8: Knit, working (k1, p1, k1) in "[yo] 3 times".

Row 9: K1, k2tog, yo twice, k2tog, k18, k2tog, yo, k2tog, k1—27 sts.

Row 11: K11, k2tog, yo twice, k2tog, k7, k2tog, yo, k2tog, k1—26 sts.

Row 13: K1, k2tog, yo twice, k2tog, k4, [k2tog, yo twice, k2tog] 2 times, k4, k2tog, yo, k2tog, k1—25 sts.

Row 15: K7, [k2tog, yo twice, k2tog] 3 times, k1, k2tog, yo, k2tog, k1—24 sts.

Row 16: K7, p1, [k3, p1] 2 times, k2tog, k6—23 sts.

Repeat Rows 1–16 for desired length. BO in knit after Row 16.

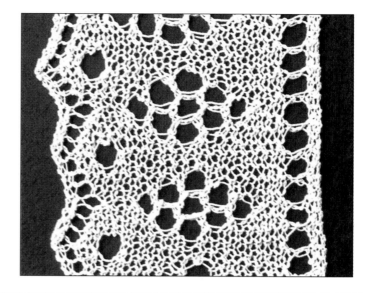

Knitted Lace #4

CO 25 sts.

Set-up row: Knit.

Row 1: K3, [k1 wrapping yarn around needle 4 times] 8 times, k2, yo twice, k2tog, k7, yo, k2tog, k1—50 sts.

Row 2: YO, k2tog, k10, p1, k2, sl the next 8 sts to the right needle, elongating them, sl them back to the left needle, pass the last 4 sts (black on chart) over the first 4 sts (gray on chart) and knit the 8 sts in that order, k3—26 sts.

Rows 3, 7, and 11: Knit to last 3

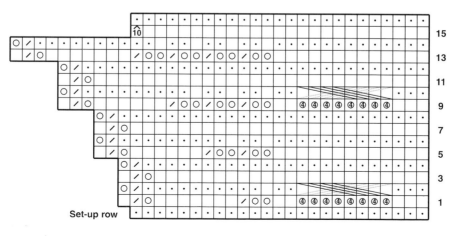

sts, yo, k2tog, k1.

Rows 4, 8, and 12: YO, k2tog, knit to end.

Row 5: K13, [yo twice, k2tog] 2 times, k6, yo, k2tog, k1—28 sts.

Row 6: YO, k2tog, k9, p1, k2, p1, k13.

Row 9: K3, [k1 wrapping yarn around needle 4 times] 8 times, k2, [yo twice, k2tog] 3 times, k6, yo, k2tog, k1—55 sts.

Row 10: YO, k2tog, k9, [p1, k2] 3 times, sl the next 8 sts to the right needle, elongating them, sl them back to the left needle, pass the last 4 sts (black on chart) over the first 4 sts (gray on chart) and knit the 8 sts in that order, k3—31 sts.

Row 13: K13, [yo twice, k2tog] 4 times, k7, yo, k2tog, k1—35 sts.

Row 14: YO, k2tog, k10, p1, [k2, p1] 3 times, k13.

Row 15: K24, pass last 10 sts on left needle over first st on left needle, k1—25 sts.

Row 16: Knit.

Repeat Rows 1–16 for desired length. BO on Row 16.

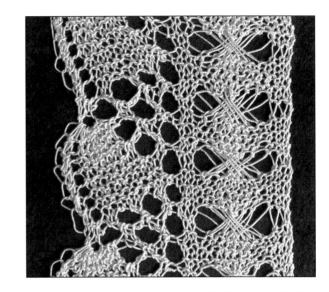

Knitted Lace #5

CO 36 sts.

Set-up row: Knit.

Row 1: K3, yo, k2tog, k1, yo, [k1, k2tog, (yo) 3 times, k2tog twice, yo, k3tog, yo] 2 times, k1, k2tog, [yo] 3 times, k2tog twice, yo,

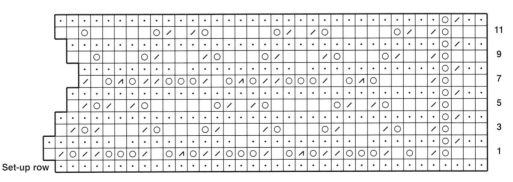

Working piece flat: rep Rows 1–12 for pattern; end Row 2.
Working piece to be grafted: end on Row 11 and graft to Row 1.

k2tog, k1—37 sts.

Row 2: K6, [p1, k9] 2 times, p1, k6, yo, k2tog, k2.

Row 3: K3, yo, k2tog, k2, [yo, k2tog, k3, k2tog, yo, k3] 2 times, yo, k2tog, k3, k2tog, yo, k2tog, k1—36 sts.

Rows 4, 6, 10, and 12: Knit to last 4 sts, yo, k2tog, k2.

Row 5: K3, yo, k2tog, k3, [yo, k2tog, k1, k2tog, yo, k5] 2 times, yo, k2tog, k1, k2tog, yo, k2tog, k1—35 sts.

Row 7: K3, yo, k2tog, k4, [yo, k3tog, yo, k1, k2tog, (yo) 3 times, k2tog twice] 2 times, yo, k3tog, yo, k1, k2tog—34 sts.

Row 8: K8, p1, k9, p1, k11, yo,

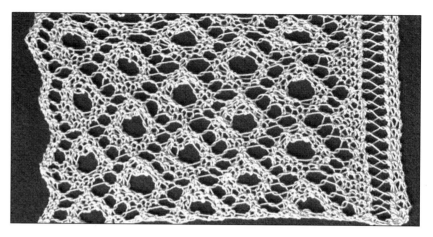

k2tog, k2.

Row 9: K3, yo, k2tog, k2, k2tog, yo, [k3, yo, k2tog, k3, k2tog, yo] 2 times, k3, yo, k2—35 sts.

Row 11: K3, yo, k2tog, [k1, k2tog,

yo, k5, yo, k2tog] 2 times, k1, k2tog, yo, k5, yo, k2—36 sts.

Repeat Rows 1–12 for desired length. BO on Row 12.

Creole Lace

CO 11 sts.

Set-up row: Knit.

Row 1: Sl 1, k1, [yo, p2tog, (k1, p1, k1, p1) in next st] 3 times—20 sts.

Row 2: [K4, yo, p2tog] 3 times, k2.

Row 3: Sl 1, k1, [yo, p2tog, k4] 3 times.

Row 4: [BO 3, yo, p2tog] 3 times, k2—11 sts.

Repeat Rows 1–4 for desired length. BO in knit after Row 4.

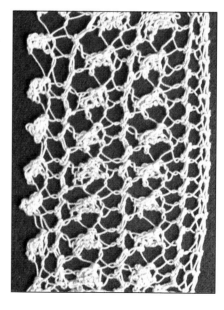

Knitted Lace #6

CO 33 sts.

Set-up row: Knit.

Row 1: Sl 1, k2, yo, p2tog, [k4, k2tog, yo, k1, yo, k2tog] 2 times, k2, [yo, k2tog] 3 times, yo, k2— 34 sts.

Rows 2, 4, 6, 8, 10, 12, and 16: Knit to last 5 sts, yo, p2tog, k3.

Row 3: Sl 1, k2, yo, p2tog, k3, [k2tog, yo, k3, yo, k2tog, k2] 2 times, [yo, k2tog] 3 times, yo, k2—35 sts.

Row 5: Sl 1, k2, yo, p2tog, k5, yo, k3tog, yo, k6, yo, k3tog, yo, k5, [yo, k2tog] 3 times, yo, k2—36 sts.

Row 7: Sl 1, k2, yo, p2tog, k23, [yo, k2tog] 3 times, yo, k2—37 sts.

Row 9: Sl 1, k2, yo, p2tog, [k4, k2tog, yo, k1, yo, k2tog] 2 times, k6, [yo, k2tog] 3 times, yo, k2— 38 sts.

Row 11: Sl 1, k2, yo, p2tog, k3, k2tog, yo, k3, yo, k2tog, k2, k2tog, yo, k3, yo, k2tog, k6, [yo, k2tog] 3 times, yo, k2—39 sts.

Row 13: Sl 1, k2, yo, p2tog, k5, yo, k3tog, yo, k6, yo, k3tog, yo, k17.

Row 14: BO 6, knit to last 5 sts, yo, p2tog, k3—33 sts.

Row 15: Sl 1, k2, yo, p2tog, k28.

Repeat Rows 1–16 for desired length. BO in knit after Row 16.

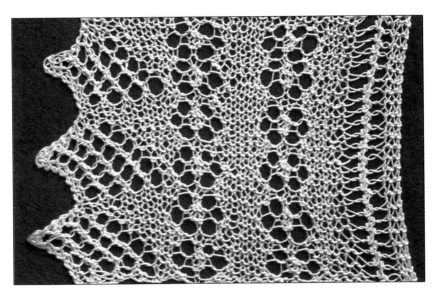

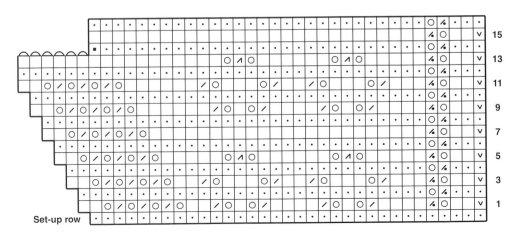

Set-up row

15

13

11

9

7

5

3

1

Leaf and Scallop Lace

CO 36 sts.

Set-up row: Knit.

Row 1: K3, yo, p2tog, k2, yo, p2tog, k3, [yo, p2tog] 4 times, k7, yo twice, k2tog, k1, [yo, p2tog] 3 times—37 sts.

Row 2: [YO, p2tog] 3 times, k3, p1, k18, yo, p2tog, k2, yo, p2tog, k3.

Row 3: K3, yo, p2tog, k2, yo, p2tog, k4, [yo, p2tog] 4 times, k10, [yo, p2tog] 3 times.

Row 4: [YO, p2tog] 3 times, k22, yo, p2tog, k2, yo, p2tog, k3.

Row 5: K3, yo, p2tog, k2, yo, p2tog, k5, [yo, p2tog] 4 times, k4, [yo twice, k2tog] 2 times, k1, [yo, p2tog] 3 times—39 sts.

Row 6: [YO, p2tog] 3 times, k3, p1, k2, p1, k17, yo, p2tog, k2, yo, p2tog, k3—39 sts.

Row 7: K3, yo, p2tog, k2, yo, p2tog, k6, [yo, p2tog] 4 times, k10, [yo, p2tog] 3 times.

Row 8: [YO, p2tog] 3 times, k24, yo, p2tog, k2, yo, p2tog, k3.

Row 9: K3, yo, p2tog, k2, yo, p2tog, k7, [yo, p2tog] 4 times, k2, [yo twice, k2tog] 3 times, k1, [yo, p2tog] 3 times—42 sts.

Row 10: [YO, p2tog] 3 times, k3, p1, [k2, p1] 2 times, k17, yo, p2tog, k2, yo, p2tog, k3.

Row 11: K3, yo, p2tog, k2, yo, p2tog, k8, [yo, p2tog] 4 times, k11, [yo, p2tog] 3 times.

Row 12: [YO, p2tog] 3 times, k27, yo, p2tog, k2, yo, p2tog, k3.

Row 13: K3, yo, p2tog, k2, yo, p2tog, k9, [yo, p2tog] 4 times, k10, [yo, p2tog] 3 times.

Row 14: K33, yo, p2tog, k2, yo, p2tog, k3.

Row 15: K3, yo, p2tog, k2, yo, p2tog, k10, [yo, p2tog] 4 times, k8, pass last 6 sts on left needle over first st on left needle, knit rem st—36 sts.

Row 16: K27, yo, p2tog, k2, yo, p2tog, k3.

Repeat Rows 1–16 for desired length. BO in knit after Row 16.

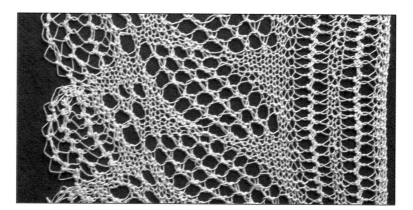

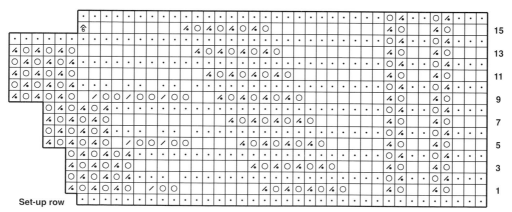

Knitted Pointed Edging #2

CO 16 sts.

Set-up row: Knit.

Row 1: [K2, yo, p2tog,] 2 times, k1, [yo, k2tog] 3 times, yo, k1—17 sts.

Row 2 and all even-numbered rows through 16: Knit to last 8 sts, [yo, p2tog, k2] 2 times.

Row 3: [K2, yo, p2tog] 2 times, k2, [yo, k2tog] 3 times, yo, k1—18 sts.

Row 5: [K2, yo, p2tog] 2 times, k3, [yo, k2tog] 3 times, yo, k1—19 sts.

Row 7: [K2, yo, p2tog] 2 times, k4, [yo, k2tog] 3 times, yo, k1—20 sts.

Row 9: [K2, yo, p2tog] 2 times, k5, [yo, k2tog] 3 times, yo, k1—21 sts.

Row 11: [K2, yo, p2tog] 2 times, k6, [yo, k2tog] 3 times, yo, k1—22 sts.

Row 13: [K2, yo, p2tog] 2 times, k7, [yo, k2tog] 3 times, yo, k1—23 sts.

Row 15: [K2, yo, p2tog] 2 times, k8, [yo, k2tog] 3 times, yo, k1—24 sts.

Row 17: [K2, yo, p2tog] 2 times, k9, [yo, k2tog] 3 times, yo, k1—25 sts.

Rows 18 and all even-numbered rows through 32: K3tog, knit to last 8 sts, [yo, p2tog, k2] 2 times.

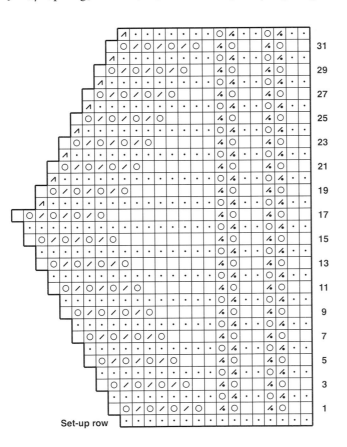

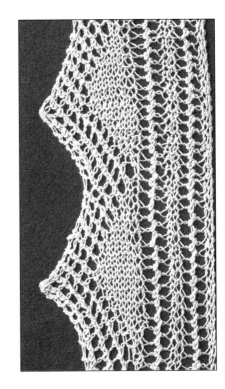

Row 19: [K2, yo, p2tog] 2 times, k7, [yo, k2tog] 3 times, yo, k1—23 sts.

Row 21: [K2, yo, p2tog] 2 times, k6, [yo, k2tog] 3 times, yo, k1—22 sts.

Row 23: [K2, yo, p2tog] 2 times, k5, [yo, k2tog] 3 times, yo, k1—21 sts.

Row 25: [K2, yo, p2tog] 2 times, k4, [yo, k2tog] 3 times, yo, k1—20 sts.

Row 27: [K2, yo, p2tog] 2 times, k3, [yo, k2tog] 3 times, yo, k1—19 sts.

Row 29: [K2, yo, p2tog] 2 times, k2, [yo, k2tog] 3 times, yo, k1—18 sts.

Row 31: [K2, yo, p2tog] 2 times, k1, [yo, k2tog] 3 times, yo, k1—17 sts.

Repeat Rows 1–32 for desired length. BO in knit after Row 32.

Mikado Lace

CO 22 sts.

Set-up row: Knit.

Row 1: K2, yo twice, k2tog, k10, [yo twice, k2tog] 3 times, k2—26 sts.

Row 2: K4, [p1, k2] 2 times, p1, k12, p1, k2.

Rows 3, 4, 7, 11, and 15: Knit.

Row 5: K2, [yo twice, k2tog] 2 times, k12, [yo twice, k2tog] 3 times, k2—31 sts.

Row 6: K4, p1, [k2, p1] 2 times, k14, [p1, k2] 2 times.

Rows 8 and 12: K2, [k2tog, k1] 8 times, k2tog, k3—22 sts.

Rows 9 and 13: K2, [yo twice, k2tog] 9 times, k2—31 sts.

Rows 10 and 14: K4, [p1, k2] 9 times.

Row 16: BO 9, k21—22 sts.

Repeat Rows 1–16 for desired length. BO on Row 16.

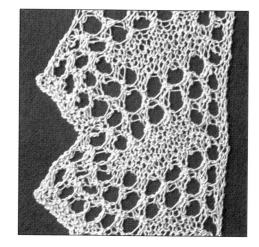

Maple Seed Lace

CO 32 sts.

Set-up row: Knit.

Row 1: Sl 1, k2, k2tog, yo twice, k2tog, k2, [yo, k2tog] 2 times, k5, yo, p3tog, yo, k5, [k2tog, yo] 2 times, p2tog—31 sts.

Row 2: YO, p1, k25, p1, k4—32 sts.

Row 3: Sl 1, k2, k2tog, yo twice, k2tog, k3, [yo, k2tog] 2 times, k3, k2tog, yo, p1, yo, k2tog, k3, [k2tog, yo] 2 times, k1, yo, p2tog.

Row 4: YO, p1, k26, p1, k4—33 sts.

Row 5: Sl 1, k2, k2tog, yo twice, k2tog, k4, [yo, k2tog] 2 times, k2, k2tog, yo, p1, yo, k2tog, k2, [k2tog, yo] 2 times, k3, yo, p2tog.

Row 6: YO, p1, k27, p1, k4—34 sts.

Row 7: Sl 1, k2, k2tog, yo twice, k2tog, k5, [yo, k2tog] 2 times, k1, k2tog, yo, p1, yo, k2tog, k1, [k2tog, yo] 2 times, k5, yo, p2tog.

Row 8: YO, p1, k28, p1, k4—35 sts.

Row 9: Sl 1, k2, k2tog, yo twice, k2tog, k6, [yo, k2tog] 2 times, k2tog, yo, p1, yo, k2tog twice, yo, k2tog, yo, k7, yo, p2tog.

Row 10: YO, p1, k29, p1, k4—36 sts.

Row 11: Sl 1, k2, k2tog, yo twice, k2tog, k4, k2tog, yo, k1, [yo, k2tog] 2 times, k3, [k2tog, yo] 2 times, k1, yo, k2tog, k4, k2tog, yo, p2tog—35 sts.

Row 12: YO, p2tog, k28, p1, k4.

Row 13: Sl 1, k2, k2tog, yo twice, k2tog, k3, [k2tog, yo] 2 times, k1, [yo, k2tog] 2 times, k1, [k2tog, yo] 2 times, k1, [yo, k2tog] 2 times, k2, k2tog, yo, p2tog—34 sts.

Row 14: YO, p2tog, k27, p1, k4.

Row 15: Sl 1, k2, k2tog, yo twice, k2tog, k2, [yo, k2tog] 2 times, k3, yo, k2tog, yo, p3tog, yo, k2tog, yo, k3, [yo, k2tog] 2 times, k2tog, yo, p2tog—33 sts.

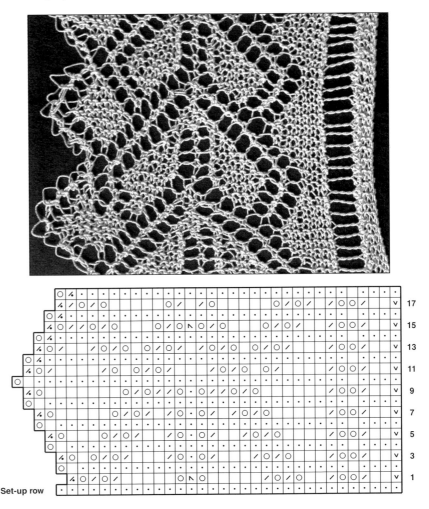

Row 16: YO, p2tog, k26, p1, k4.

Row 17: Sl 1, k2, k2tog, yo twice, k2tog, k1, [k2tog, yo] 2 times, k5, yo, k2tog, k1, k2tog, yo, k5, [yo, k2tog] 2 times, p2tog—31 sts.

Row 18: YO, p2tog, k25, p1, k4—32 sts.

Repeat Rows 1–18 for desired length. BO in knit after Row 18.

Fancy Scallop Edging

CO 21 sts.

Set-up row: Knit.

Row 1: K11, [yo, k2tog] 2 times, [yo] 4 times, k2tog twice, yo, k2tog—23 sts.

Row 2: K4, (k1, p1, k1, p1) in "[yo] 4 times", k15.

Row 3: K5, k2tog, yo twice, k2tog, k3, [yo, k2tog] 2 times, k4, k2tog, yo, k1.

Row 4: K16, p1, k6.

Row 5: K3, [k2tog, yo twice, k2tog] 2 times, k2, [yo, k2tog] 2 times, k3, k2tog, yo, k1.

Row 6: K14, p1, k3, p1, k4.

Row 7: K5, k2tog, yo twice, k2tog, k5, [yo, k2tog] 2 times, k2, k2tog, yo, k1.

Row 8: K16, p1, k6.

Row 9: K3, [k2tog, yo twice, k2tog] 2 times, k4, [yo, k2tog] 2 times, k1, k2tog, yo, k1.

Row 10: K14, p1, k3, p1, k4.

Row 11: K5, k2tog, yo twice, k2tog, k7, [yo, k2tog] 2 times, k2tog, yo, k1.

Row 12: K16, p1, k6.

Row 13: K17, [yo, k2tog] 2 times, slip the last st back to the left needle, pass the last 2 sts over the first st, place st back on right needle—21 sts.

Row 14: Knit.

Repeat Rows 1–14 for desired length. BO on Row 14.

Knitted Lace #7

CO 27 sts.

Set-up row: Knit.

Row 1: Sl 1, k2, yo, k2tog, k1, yo, k2tog, k3, k2tog, yo, k1, yo, ssk, k5, k2tog, yo, k1, yo, ssk, k1.

Row 2 and all even-numbered rows: Knit to last 3 sts, yo, k2tog, k1.

Row 3: Sl 1, k2, yo, k2tog, k1, yo, k2tog, k2, k2tog, yo, k3, yo, ssk, k3, k2tog, yo, k3, yo, k2—28 sts.

Row 5: Sl 1, k2, [yo, k2tog, k1] 2 times, [k2tog, yo] 2 times, k1, [yo, ssk] 2 times, k1, [k2tog, yo] 2 times, k1, yo, ssk, yo, k2—29 sts.

Row 7: Sl 1, k2, yo, k2tog, k1, yo, k2tog twice, yo, k2tog, yo, k3, yo, ssk, yo, sl 1, k2tog, psso, yo, k2tog, yo, k3, yo, ssk, yo, k2—30 sts.

Row 9: Sl 1, k2, [yo, k2tog, k1] 2 times, [yo, k2tog, yo, ssk, k1, k2tog, yo, ssk, yo, k1] 2 times, k1.

Row 11: Sl 1, k2, yo, k2tog, k1, yo, k2tog, k2, yo, ssk, yo, sl 1, k2tog, psso, yo, k2tog, yo, k3, yo, ssk, yo, sl 1, k2tog, psso, [yo, k2tog] 2 times, k1—29 sts.

Row 13: Sl 1, k2, yo, k2tog, k1, yo, k2tog, k3, yo, ssk, k1, k2tog, yo, k5, yo, ssk, k1, k2tog, yo, k2tog, k1—28 sts.

Row 15: Sl 1, k2, yo, k2tog, k1, yo, k2tog, k4, yo, sl 1, k2tog, psso, yo, k7, yo, sl 1, k2tog, psso, yo, k2tog, k1—27 sts.

Repeat Rows 1–16 for desired length. BO in knit after Row 16.

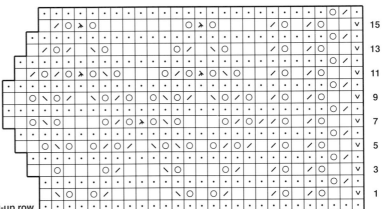

PROJECTS

Knitted Lace Tablecloth with Mitered Corners

A purchased hemstitched tablecloth is edged with Knitted Lace #7. The lace is worked in strips, beginning and ending at the corners, and then sewn onto a foundation row of single crochet worked into the hemstitching.

Thread: Coats Patons Opera, size 10: 4 balls.

Needles: Size 3 (3.25 mm).

Notions: Size 6 (1.8 mm) steel crochet hook; hemstitched tablecloth; matching sewing thread; sewing needle.

Lace strips: (Make 4)

Beg mitered corner: CO 23 sts. Knit to last 3 sts, then proceed as follows:

Row 1: Sl 1, yo, k2.

Row 2: K5, turn.

Row 3: Sl 1, k2, yo, k2.

Row 4: K7, turn.

Row 5: Sl 1, [k1, yo] 2 times, k2tog, yo, k2.

Row 6: K10, turn.

Row 7: Sl 1, k2tog, yo, k3, yo, k2tog, yo, k2.

Row 8: K12, turn.

Row 9: Sl 1, yo, k2tog, yo, ssk, k1, [k2tog, yo] 2 times, k2.

Rows 10, 12, 14, and 16: K13, turn.

Row 11: Sl 1, k2, yo, ssk, yo, sl 1, k2tog, psso, [yo, k2tog] 2 times, k1.

Row 13: Sl 1, k4, yo, ssk, k1, k2tog, yo, k2tog, k1.

Row 15: Sl 1, k6, yo, sl 1, k2tog, psso, yo, k2tog, k1.

Row 17: Sl 1, k6, k2tog, yo, k1, yo, k2tog, k1.

Row 18: K14, turn.

Row 19: Sl 1, k1, yo, ssk, k3, k2tog, yo, k3, yo, k2.

Row 20: K16, turn.

Row 21: Sl 1, k1, [yo, ssk] 2 times, k1, [k2tog, yo] 2 times, k1, yo, ssk, yo, k2.

Row 22: K18, turn.

Row 23: Sl 1, k3, yo, ssk, yo, sl 1, k2tog, psso, yo, k2tog, yo, k3, yo, ssk, yo, k2.

Row 24: K20, turn.

Row 25: Sl 1, yo, k2tog, k1, k2tog, yo, ssk, yo, k1, yo, k2tog, yo, ssk, k1, k2tog, yo, ssk, yo k2.

Rows 26, 28, 30, and 32: K21, turn.

Row 27: Sl 1, yo, ssk, yo, sl 1, k2tog, psso, yo, k2tog, yo, k3, yo, ssk, yo, sl 1, k2tog, psso, [yo, k2tog] 2 times, k1.

Row 29: Sl 1, k2, yo, ssk, k1, k2tog, yo, k5, yo, ssk, k1, k2tog, yo, k2tog, k1.

Row 31: Sl 1, k4, yo, sl 1, k2tog, psso, yo, k7, yo, sl 1, k2tog, psso, yo, k2tog, k1.

Row 33: Sl 1, k4, k2tog, yo, k1, yo, ssk, k5, k2tog, yo, k1, yo, k2tog, k1.

Row 34: K22, turn.

Row 35: Sl 1, yo, k2tog, k2, k2tog, yo, k3, yo, ssk, k3, k2tog, yo, k3, yo, k2.

Row 36: K24, turn.

Row 37: Sl 1, k1, yo, k2tog, k1, [k2tog, yo] 2 times, k1, [yo, ssk] 2 times, k1, [k2tog, yo] 2 times, k1, yo, ssk, yo, k2.

Row 38: K26, turn.

Row 39: Sl 1, k2, yo, k2tog twice, yo, k2tog, yo, k3, yo, ssk, yo, sl 1, k2tog, psso, yo, k2tog, yo, k3, yo, ssk, yo, k2.

Row 40: K28, turn.

Row 41: Sl 1, [yo, k2tog, k1] 2 times, yo, k2tog, yo, ssk, k1, k2tog, yo, ssk, yo, k1, yo, k2tog, yo, ssk, k1, k2tog, yo, ssk, yo, k2.

Row 42: K27, yo, k1.

Row 43: Sl 1, [k1, yo, k2tog] 2 times, k1, yo, ssk, yo, sl 1, k2tog, psso, yo, k2tog, yo, k3, yo, ssk, yo, sl 1, k2tog, psso, [yo, k2tog] 2 times, k1.

Row 44: K26, yo, k2.

Row 45: Sl 1, k2, yo, k2tog, k1, yo, k2tog, k3, yo, ssk, k1, k2tog, yo, k5, yo, ssk, k1, k2tog, yo, k2tog, k1.

Row 46: K25, yo, k2tog, k1.

Row 47: Sl 1, k2, yo, k2tog, k1, yo, k2tog, k4, yo, sl 1, k2tog, psso, yo, k7, yo, sl 1, k2tog, psso, yo, k2tog, k1.

Row 48: K24, yo, k2tog, k1—3 scallops formed; 27 sts on needle.

Straight edge: Repeat Rows 1–16 of Knitted Lace #7 (see page 72) until straight edge of border is slightly shorter than edge of tablecloth to allow for stretch.

End mitered corner:

Rows 1–6: Work Rows 1–6 of straight edge pattern.

Row 7: Ssk, k1, yo, k2tog, k1, yo, k2tog twice, yo, k2tog, yo, k3, yo, ssk, yo, sl 1, k2tog, psso, yo, k2tog, yo, k3, yo, ssk, yo, k2.

Row 8: K27, yo, k2tog.

Row 9: Ssk, [yo, k2tog, k1] 2 times, yo, k2tog, yo, ssk, k1, k2tog, yo, ssk, yo, k1, yo, k2tog, yo, ssk, k1, k2tog, yo, ssk, yo, k2.

Row 10: K28.

Row 11: Ssk, k2, yo, k2tog, k2, yo, ssk, yo, sl 1, k2tog, psso, yo, k2tog, yo, k3, yo, ssk, yo, sl 1, k2tog, psso, [yo, k2tog] 2 times, k1.

Row 12: K26.

Row 13: Sl 1, k1, psso, k1, yo, k2tog, k3, yo, ssk, k1, k2tog, yo, k5, yo, ssk, k1, k2tog, yo, k2tog, k1.

Row 14: K24.

Row 15: Ssk, yo, k2tog, k4, yo, sl 1, k2tog, psso, yo, k7, yo, sl 1, k2tog, psso, yo, k2tog, k1.

Row 16: K22.

Row 17: Ssk, k4, k2tog, yo, k1, yo, ssk, k5, yo, k1, yo, k2tog, k1, k2tog.

Rows 18, 20, and 22: K21.

Row 19: Ssk, k2, k2tog, yo, k3, yo, ssk, k3, k2tog, yo, k3, yo, k2.

Row 21: Ssk, [k2tog, yo] 2 times, k1, [yo, ssk] 2 times, k1, [k2tog, yo] 2 times, k1, yo, ssk, yo, k2.

Row 23: Ssk, yo, k2tog, yo, k3, yo, ssk, yo, sl 1, k2tog, psso, yo, k2tog, yo, k3, yo, ssk, yo, k2.

Row 24: K22.

Row 25: Sl 1, k2tog, psso, yo, ssk, k1, k2tog, yo, ssk, yo, k1, yo, k2tog, yo, ssk, k1, k2tog, yo, ssk, yo, k2.

Row 26: K20.

Row 27: Ssk, sl 1, k2tog, psso, yo, k2tog, yo, k3, yo, ssk, yo, sl 1, k2tog, psso, [yo, k2tog] 2 times, k1.

Row 28: K17.

Row 29: Ssk, k2tog, yo, k5, yo, ssk, k1, k2tog, yo, k2tog, k1.

Row 30: K15.

Row 31: Ssk, yo, k7, yo, sl 1, k2tog, psso, yo, k2tog, k1.

Row 32: K14.

Row 33: Sl 1, k2tog, psso, k5, k2tog, yo, k1, yo, k2tog, k1.

Rows 34, 36, 38, and 40: K12.

Row 35: Ssk, k3, k2tog, yo, k3, yo, k2.

Row 37: Ssk, k1, [k2tog, yo] 2 times, k1, yo, ssk, yo, k2.

Row 39: Sl 1, k2tog, psso, yo, k2tog, yo, k3, yo, ssk, yo, k2.

Row 41: Sl 1, k2tog, psso, yo, ssk, k1, k2tog, yo, ssk, yo, k2.

Row 42: K10.

Row 43: Ssk, yo, sl 1, k2tog, psso, [yo, k2tog] 2 times, k1.

Row 44: K8.

Row 45: Ssk, k1, k2tog, yo, k2tog, k1.

Row 46: K6.

Row 47: Sl 1, k2tog, psso, yo, k2tog, k1.

Row 48: K4.

Row 49: Ssk, k2.

Row 50: K3.

Row 51: Sl 1, k2tog, psso. Finish off.

Finishing: Beg in the middle of one edge of tablecloth, work 1 row sc into hemstitching, working 4 sc in each corner. Join with slip st. Finish off. Block borders so that straight edge measures the same as the edge of the tablecloth. With matching thread, sew the borders to each side of the tablecloth. Sew mitered corners together, matching patterns. Block.

Handkerchiefs
(Shown on page 76)

Fine lace borders the edges of two purchased handkerchiefs. A foundation of single crochet worked into the hemstitching allows the edging to be attached while it is knitted. The beginning and ending stitches are grafted together inconspicuously along one edge. The handkerchief on the right is edged with a variation of Knitted Lace #1 (see page 26); the handkerchief on the left with Narrow Knitted Edging (see page 28).

Knitted Lace Edging

Thread: Size 20 crochet cotton (MC): 1 ball.

Needles: Size 00 (1.75 mm).

Notions: Linen handkerchief square with hemstitching; waste thread in contrasting color; size 7 (1.65 mm) steel crochet hook; tapestry needle.

Preparation: Beg in the middle of one side of the handkerchief, work 1 row sc into hemstitching, working 4 sc into each corner. Join with a slip st. Cut thread and finish off. Set aside.

Edging: With waste thread, CO 12 sts. Knit 4 rows. Change to MC. K11, sl 1, k1, psso with last st and first sc on border—12 sts. *Note:* Slip all sts pwise with thread in front.

Knitted Lace Handkerchiefs

Row 1: Sl 1, k1, yo, k2tog, k3, k2tog, yo, k1, yo k2—13 sts.

Row 2 and all even-numbered rows: Knit to last st, sl 1, k1, psso with next st of sc.

Row 3: Sl 1, k1, yo, k2tog, k2, k2tog, yo, k3, yo, k2—14 sts.

Row 5: Sl 1, k1, yo, k2tog, k1, k2tog, yo, k5, yo, k2—15 sts.

Row 7: Sl 1, k1, yo, k2tog, k3, yo, k2tog, k1, k2tog, yo, k2tog, k1—14 sts.

Row 9: Sl 1, k1, yo, k2tog, k4, yo, sl 1, k2tog, psso, yo, k2tog, k1—13 sts.

Row 11: Sl 1, k1, yo, k2tog, k4, k2tog, yo, k2tog, k1—12 sts.

Rep Rows 1–12, attaching knitted edging to sc around handkerchief as you go, working corners as follows. *Corners:* Work to 12 sc's from corner, [sl 1, k1, psso] 2 times into each sc (doubling the number of rows into each sc will allow the corner to lie flat). Rep for 12 sc after corner. Cont in this manner around handkerchief, ending with Row 11. (Skip 1 sc or work 2 sc in the same space if necessary to make knitted edging fit the number of sc's on the handkerchief.) Do not BO. Remove waste thread and place live sts on needle. Cut thread and use it to graft beg sts to end sts. Weave in loose ends. Block.

Narrow Knitted Edging

Thread: Size 40 crochet thread: 1 ball.

Needles: Size 0000 (1.25 mm).

Notions: Linen handkerchief square with hemstitching; size 9 (1.4 mm) steel crochet hook; sewing needle.

Preparation: Beg in the middle of one side, work 1 row sc into hemstitching, working 4 sc into each corner. Join with a slip st. Cut thread and finish off. Set aside.

Edging: CO 9 st. Knit 1 row. Repeat Rows 1–12 of Narrow Knitted Edging (see page 28) until border fits around handkerchief, slightly stretched, ending with Row 11 and allowing 2 points for each corner and the same number of points for each straight edge. BO on Row 12.

Finishing: Graft ends together. With crochet thread on a fine needle, sew edging to sc crochet edge. Weave in loose ends. Block.

Baby Sweater and Hat

Mrs. Belli's Diamond Edging (page 28) borders the edges and collar of this knitted baby sweater. The sweater is knitted in one piece from the bottom up. The collar and sleeves are worked separately and sewn in place.

Finished size: *Sweater:* 19½ [21, 22½]" (49.5 [53.5, 57] cm) chest circumference; to fit 6 months (1, 2) years; *Hat:* 16 (17½, 18¾)" (40.5 [44.5, 47.5] cm) circumference.

Yarn: Tahki Cotton Classic (109 yd [100 m]/50 g): *Sweater:* 4 (5, 6) skeins; *Hat:* 1 (2, 2) skeins.

Needles: Size 5 and 6 (3.75 and 4 mm): *Sweater:* 24" (60 cm) circular (cir); *Hat:* 16" (40 cm) cir and size 6 (4 mm) double-pointed (dpn). Adjust needle size if necessary to obtain the correct gauge.

Notions: Stitch holders; tapestry needle; four 1/2" (11.5 cm) buttons; waste yarn.

Gauge: 10 sts and 14 rows = 2" (5 cm) in St st on larger needle; 4 pattern repeats = 5" (12.5 cm) in border st on smaller needle.

Sweater

Body: *Border:* With smaller cir needle, CO 9 sts. Knit 1 row. Work Rows 1–12 of Mrs. Belli's Diamond Edging (see page 28) 16 (17, 18) times, ending with Row 11 of last rep. BO in patt following Row 12. Do not finish off. Place rem st on larger cir needle, and with same needle, pick up and knit 97 (103, 111) sts along the straight edge of the border— 98 (104, 112) sts total. *Body:* Knit 3 rows. Beg with a knit row, work St st until piece measures 4½ (5½, 6½)" (11.5 [14, 16.5] cm) from pick-up edge, ending with a WS row. *Divide for fronts and back:* Work across 18 (20, 22) sts for right front, place 50 (52, 56) sts

for back and rem 30 (32, 34) sts for left front on holder. ***Right front: Shape V-neck:*** Dec 1 st at neck edge on next and every foll 2 rows 4 (5, 6) times total, then every 4 rows 4 (5, 5) times—10 (10, 11) sts rem. Cont even until armhole measures 4 (4½, 4¾)" (10 [11.5, 12] cm). Place sts on holder. ***Back:*** Place 50 (52, 56) held back sts on needle. With RS facing, join yarn, BO 12 sts, and work to end of row—38 (40, 44) sts rem. Cont even until armhole measures same as front. Place sts on holders as follows: 10 (10, 11) sts for each shoulder and 18 (20, 22) sts for back neck. ***Left front:*** Place 30 (32, 34) left front sts on needle. With RS facing, join yarn, BO 12 sts, and work to end of row, and *at the same time,* shape neck as for right front—10 (10, 11) sts rem. Cont even until armhole measures same as back. Place sts on holder.

Sleeves: With smaller cir needle, CO 9 sts. Knit 1 row. Work Rows 1–12 of Mrs. Belli's Diamond Edging 5 (5, 6) times, and BO in patt on last rep of Row 12. Do not finish off. Place rem st on larger needle, and with same needle, pick up and knit 30 (30, 36) sts across straight edge of border—31 (31, 37) sts total. Knit 3 rows. Beg with a knit row, work St st, inc 1 st each

end of needle every 4 rows 5 (7, 6) times—41 (45, 49) sts. Cont even until piece measures 5 (5½, 6¼)" (12.5 [14, 16] cm) from pick-up edge. ***Shape cap:*** BO 4 (4, 5) sts at beg of next 2 rows. BO 4 (5, 5) sts at beg of next 2 rows. BO 4 (5, 6) sts at beg of next 2 rows. BO rem 17 sts.

Finishing: Place 10 (10, 11) back shoulder sts on one needle and 10 (10, 11) front shoulder sts on another needles. Using a third needle, BO the shoulder sts tog. Rep for other shoulder. ***Front bands:*** With smaller cir needle and beg at lower right front edge, pick up and knit 35 (41, 47) sts to base of neck shaping and 33 (37, 41) sts to shoulder seam, knit across 18 (20, 22) held back neck sts, and pick up and knit 33 (37, 41) sts to base of left front neck shaping and 35 (41, 47) sts to lower left front edge—154 (176, 198) sts total. Knit 3 rows. *Buttonhole row:* K4, (k2tog, yo, k7 [9, 11]) 3 times, k2tog, yo, knit to end of row. Knit 3 rows. BO loosely. ***Collar:*** With smaller cir needle, CO 9 sts. Knit 1 row. Work Rows 1–12 of Mrs. Belli's Diamond Edging 12 (13, 14) times, ending last rep with Row 11. BO in patt following Row 12. With yarn threaded on a tapestry needle,

sew collar to neck opening between base of V-neck on both fronts and around back neck. Weave in loose ends. Sew buttons opposite buttonholes.

- - - - - - - - - - - - - - -

Hat

With waste yarn and smaller cir needle, CO 9 sts. Knit 4 rows. Change to main yarn. Work Rows 1–12 of Mrs. Belli's Diamond Edging (see page 28) 13 (14, 15) times. Remove waste yarn and graft sts tog. Finish off. With larger cir needle, pick up and knit 80 (86, 92) sts around straight edge of border. Place marker and join. Purl 1 rnd. Knit 1 rnd, inc 0 (2, 4) sts evenly spaced—80, (88, 96) sts. Purl 1 rnd. Cont in St st until piece measures 1½ (2, 2½)" (3.8 [5, 6.5] cm) from pick-up rnd, changing to dpn when necessary. ***Shape top:***
Rnd 1: [K6 (7, 8), ssk, yo, k2tog] 8 times—72 (80, 88) sts.
Rnd 2 and all even-numbered rnds: Knit.
Rnd 3: [K5 (6, 7), ssk, yo, k2tog] 8 times—64 (72, 80) sts.
Rnd 5: [K4 (5, 6), ssk, yo, k2tog] 8 times—56 (64, 72) sts.
Rnd 7: [K3 (4, 5), ssk, yo, k2tog] 8 times—48 (56, 64) sts.
Rnd 9: [K2 (3, 4), ssk, yo, k2tog] 8

times—40 (48, 56) sts.

Rnd 11: [K1 (2, 3), ssk, yo, k2tog] 8 times—32 (40, 48) sts.

Rnd 13: [k0 (1, 2), ssk, yo, k2tog] 8 times—24 (32, 40) sts.

Rnd 15: [k0 (0, 1), ssk, yo, k2tog] 8

times—18 (24, 32) sts.

Rnd 17: For small size only: Sl 1, k2tog, psso—6 sts. Finish off. *For medium (large) sizes:* [Ssk, yo, k2tog] 6 (8) times—18 (24) sts.

Rnd 19: For medium size only: Work Rnd 17 as for small size. *For large size:* [Ssk, yo, k2tog] 6 times—18 sts.

Rnd 21: For large size only: Work Rnd 17 as for small size.

Baby Hat and Booties

Combination Lace creates the border of the baby hat. The lace is knitted in a strip from one side, over the top of the head, and to the other side. Stitches are picked up along the straight edge of the lace and the lace is worked in short rows to shape the back of the hat. The neckband is worked downward from picked-up stitches. Ribbon is threaded through eyelets for the tie. The booties are worked in the round on double-pointed needles. The lace cuffs are worked sideways and stitches are picked up along the straight edge of the lace as for the hat, then worked downward for the foot. The ribbon ties are threaded through eyelet holes.

Finished size: To fit 6 months to 1 year.

Yarn: 2 ply Hunt Valley 100% Cashmere (100 yd [91 m]/ 1/2 oz): **Hat:** 1/2 oz; **Booties:** 1/4 oz.

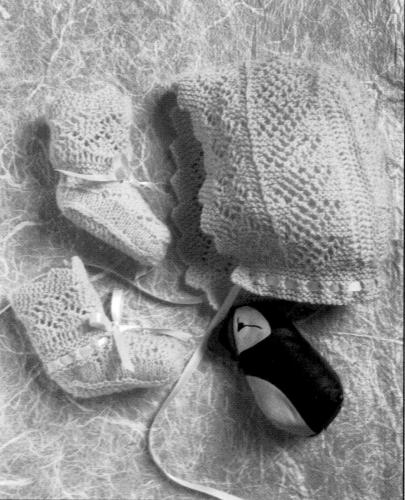

Needles: *Hat:* Size 3 (3.25 mm): straight; *Booties:* Size 2 and 3 (2.75 and 3.25 mm): double-pointed (dpn). Adjust needle size if necessary to obtain the correct gauge.

Notions: Stitch holder; marker; about 1 yd (1 m) of 1/4" (6 mm) satin ribbon each for hat and booties; tapestry needle.

Gauge: *Hat:* 2 repeats of lace pattern = 1¾" (4.5 cm) on larger needles; *Booties:* 14 sts and 28 rows = 2" (5 cm) in garter st on larger needles; 2 repeats of bootie border = 2" (5 cm) on smaller needles.

– · – · – · – · – · – · – · – · –

Hat

With smaller needles, work Rows 1–12 of Combination Lace (see page 55) 14 times, and BO on last rep of Row 12. Do not finish off—1 st rem on needle. With same needle and WS of lace facing, pick up and knit 85 sts along straight edge of lace—86 sts total. Knit 1 row. **Short-row shape back:** *Note:* Sl sts pwise with yarn in front.
Set-up row: (WS) K53, ssk, turn.
Row 1: (RS) Sl 1, k3, yo, k2tog, k1, [yo, k2tog] 3 times, k5, yo, k2tog, k1, p2tog, turn.
Row 2 and all even-numbered rows: Sl 1, k3, yo, k2tog, k12, yo,

k2tog, k1, ssk, turn.
Row 3: Sl 1, k3, yo, k2tog, k2, [yo, k2tog] 3 times, k4, yo, k2tog, k1, p2tog, turn.
Row 5: Sl 1, k3, yo, k2tog, k3, [yo, k2tog] 3 times, k3, yo, k2tog, k1, p2tog, turn.
Row 7: Sl 1, k3, yo, k2tog, k4, [yo, k2tog] 3 times, k2, yo, k2tog, k1, p2tog, turn.
Row 9: Sl 1, k3, yo, k2tog, k5, [yo, k2tog] 3 times, k1, yo, k2tog, k1, p2tog, turn.
Row 11: Sl 1, k3, yo, k2tog, k6, [yo, k2tog] 4 times, k1, p2tog, turn.
Work Rows 1–12 four more times.
Next row: K3, k2tog, k12, k2tog, k1, p2tog, turn. *Next row:* Sl 1, k3, k2tog, k7, k2tog, k2, ssk, turn. *Next row:* Sl 1, k13, p2tog. Place rem 15 sts on holder. Cut yarn.

Neckband: With smaller needle and RS facing, pick up and knit 28 sts along left bottom edge, knit 15 held sts, and pick up and knit 27 sts along right bottom edge—70 sts. Knit 5 rows. *Eyelet row:* K3, [yo, k2tog] 32 times, yo, k3. Knit 4 rows. BO loosely. Insert ribbon through eyelets.

– · – · – · – · – · – · – · – · –

Booties

Border: With smaller needles, CO 13 sts.
Row 1: K1, yo, k2tog, k3, yo, k1, yo, k6—15 sts.

Row 2, 4, 6, 10 and 12: Knit.
Row 3: K1, yo, k2tog, k1, k2tog, yo, k3, yo, k6—16 sts.
Row 5: K1, yo, k2tog twice, yo, k5, yo, k6—17 sts.
Row 7: K1, yo, k3tog, yo, k2tog, k3, k2tog, yo, k6—16 sts.
Row 8: BO 3 sts, knit to end—13 sts.
Row 9: K1, [yo, k2tog, k1] 2 times, k2tog, yo, k4.
Row 11: K1, yo, k2tog, k2, yo, sl 1, k2tog, psso, yo, k5.
Work Rows 1–12 six times, ending last rep with Row 12. Cut yarn and graft live sts to CO edge to form a ring. With larger needles and RS facing, pick up and knit 37 sts along straight edge of border. Distribute sts evenly onto 3 dpn. Place marker and join. Purl 1 rnd, [knit 1 rnd, purl 1 rnd] 2 times. *Eyelet rnd:* K1, [yo, k2tog] to end of rnd, yo—38 sts. Purl 1 rnd. Knit 1 rnd. Purl 1 rnd. Working last 12 sts only, redistribute rem sts to other needles. Turn, p12.

Instep:
Row 1: K1, [yo, k2tog] 3 times, k5.
Row 2 and all even-numbered rows: Knit.
Row 3: K2, [yo, k2tog] 3 times, k4.
Row 5: K3, [yo, k2tog] 3 times, k3.
Row 7: K4, [yo, k2tog] 3 times, k2.
Row 9: K5, [yo, k2tog] 3 times, k1.
Row 11: K6, [yo, k2tog] 3 times.
Repeat Rows 1–12 once. K12, pick

up and knit 11 sts along left side of instep, knit 26 sts on needles, pick up and knit 11 sts along right side of instep—60 sts. Place marker for beg of rnd. Knit 6 rnds. *Shape sole:* K11, *ssk, turn, sl 1, k10, p2tog, turn, sl 1, k10; rep from * until 12 sts rem at back of bootie—24 sts total. Graft heel sts tog. Insert ribbon through eyelets.

Hand Towels

Ordinary terrycloth towels become designer accents with knitted lace edgings. The towel on the left is edged with eight repeats of Hilton Lace (see page 31); the towel on the right is edged with four repeats of Knitted Pointed Edging #2 (see page 68). The lace is sewn by hand to the towels.

Thread: Size 10 crochet cotton in color to match towel.
Needles: Size 2 (2.75 mm).
Notions: Size 6 (1.8 mm) steel crochet hook; tapestry needle; terry cloth towel.

Preparation: Work 1 row of slip st into flat border area of fingertip towel where lace is to be attached. Finish off.

Edging: CO and work the pattern of your choice (choose one with a straight edge) until piece

measures same as towel width when slightly stretched. BO loosely.

Finishing: Block edging to width of towel. Sew edging to towel along crochet edge. Weave in loose ends.

If desired, trim the fringe under the lace border and work a small rolled hem to finish the edge.

Linen Towels

Commercially available hem-stitched fine linen towels are accented with knitted lace trim. Heart Lace #2 (see page 40) is used on the towel on the right; Maple Seed Lace (see page 70) is used on the towel on the left. The edgings are knitted in strips, then sewn to the hems of the towels.

Thread: Size 10 crochet cotton.
Needles: Size 3 (3.25 mm).
Notions: Linen towels with hem-stitching; size 6 (1.8 mm) steel crochet hook; sewing needle.

Preparation: Work 1 row of sc into hemstitching. Finish off.

Edging: CO and work the pattern of your choice (choose one with a straight edge) until piece measures same as towel width when slightly stretched. BO loosely.

Finishing: Block edging to width of towel. With crochet cotton threaded on a needle, sew edging to sc on towel. Weave in loose ends.

Fan Lace Short-Row Doily

This doily, worked in Fan Lace, is shaped with short rows and can be worked on straight knitting needles. The stitches at the beginning edge are grafted to the stitches at the ending edge to form a circle.

Thread: Size 5 crochet cotton (MC): 1 ball.
Needles: Size 3 (3.25 mm).
Notions: Small amount of waste thread in contrasting color; marker; tapestry needle.
Note: Slip marker on each row.

With waste thread, CO 24 sts. Knit 4 rows. Change to MC. Knit 1 row.

Row 1: Sl 1 wyb, k11, place marker, k2, yo twice, k2tog, k4, k2tog, yo, k2.

Row 2: YO, k2tog, k8, p1, k13, turn.

Row 3: Sl 1 wyb, knit to marker, k9, k2tog, yo, k2.

Row 4: YO, k2tog, k21, turn.

Row 5: Sl 1 wyb, knit to marker, k2, [yo twice, k2tog] 2 times, k3, k2tog, yo, k2.

Row 6: YO, k2tog, k7, [p1, k2] 2 times, k9, turn.

Row 7: Sl 1 wyb, knit to marker, k11, k2tog, yo, k2.

Row 8: YO, k2tog, k21, turn.

Row 9: Sl 1 wyb, knit to marker, k2, [yo twice, k2tog] 3 times, k3, k2tog, yo, k2.

Row 10: YO, k2tog, k7, [p1, k2] 3 times, k9, turn.

Row 11: Sl 1 wyb, knit to marker, k11 (7 sts rem on left needle), pass 5 sts on left needle over 1st st, k2tog.

Row 12: YO, k2tog, k16, turn.

Row 13: Sl 1 wyb, knit to marker, k2, yo twice, k2tog, k4, k2tog, yo, k2.

Row 14: YO, k2tog, k8, p1, k7, turn.

Row 15: Sl 1 wyb, knit to marker, k9, k2tog, yo, k2.

Row 16: YO, k2tog, k15, turn.

Row 17: Sl 1 wyb, knit to marker, k2, [yo twice, k2tog] 2 times, k3, k2tog, yo, k2.

Row 18: YO, k2tog, k7, [p1, k2] 2 times, k5, turn.

Row 19: Sl 1 wyb, knit to marker, k11, k2tog, yo, k2.

Row 20: YO, k2tog, k15, turn.

Row 21: Sl 1 wyb, knit to marker, k2, [yo twice, k2tog] 3 times, k3, k2tog, yo, k2.

Row 22: YO, k2tog, k7, [p1, k2] 3 times, k1, turn.

Row 23: Sl 1 wyb, k11 (7 sts rem on left needle), pass 5 sts on left needle over 1st st, k2tog.

Row 24: YO, k2tog, knit. Turn. Repeat Rows 1–24 nine times

more, but do not turn on last rep of Row 24. Remove waste thread and graft live sts to beg sts to form a circle. Weave in loose ends, closing up hole in center. Block.

Fairy Lace Doily

The border of this doily is worked in a strip and grafted into a circle. Stitches are picked up around the inner edge of the loop and the rest of the doily is worked in the round to the center.

Thread: Size 10 crochet cotton: 1 ball (MC).

Needles: Size 3 (3.25 mm): 16" circular (cir) and set of 4 double-pointed (dpn).

Notions: Small amount of waste thread in contrasting color; markers; tapestry needle.

Border: With cir needle and waste thread, CO 12 sts, Knit 4 rows. Change to MC and knit 1 row. Work Rows 1–4 of Fairy Lace (see page 32) 60 times. Do not BO. Remove waste thread and graft ends tog to form a circle.

With cir needle, pick up and knit 1 st from each loop on straight edge of border—120 sts. Place marker. Knit 1 rnd. Purl 1 rnd. Knit 1 rnd. K14, k2tog, [k28, k2tog] 3 times, k14—116 sts. Place marker every 29 sts for corners.

Note: Change to dpn when necessary.

Rnd 1: ([SSK, yo] 6 times, k1, sl 2

sts tog kwise, k1, p2sso, k1, [yo, k2tog] 6 times) 4 times—27 sts each section.

Rnd 2 and even-numbered rnds through 26: Knit.

Rnd 3: ([SSK, yo] 6 times, sl 2 sts tog kwise, k1, p2sso, [yo, k2tog] 6 times) 4 times—25 sts in each section.

Rnd 5: ([SSK, yo] 5 times, k1, sl 2 sts tog kwise, k1, p2sso, k1, [yo, k2tog] 5 times) 4 times—23 sts each section.

Rnd 7: ([SSK, yo] 5 times, sl 2 sts tog kwise, k1, p2sso, [yo, k2tog] 5 times) 4 times—21 sts each section.

Rnd 9: ([SSK, yo] 4 times, k1, sl 2 sts tog kwise, k1, p2sso, k1, [yo,

k2tog] 6 times) 4 times—19 sts each section.

Rnd 11: ([SSK, yo] 4 times, sl 2 sts tog kwise, p2sso, [yo, k2tog] 6 times) 4 times—17 sts each section.

Rnd 13: ([SSK, yo] 3 times, k1, sl 2 sts tog kwise, k1, p2sso, k1, [yo, k2tog] 3 times) 4 times—15 sts each section.

Rnd 15: ([SSK, yo] 3 times, sl 2 sts tog kwise, k1, p2sso, [yo, k2tog] 3 times) 4 times—13 sts each section.

Rnd 17: ([SSK, yo] 2 times, k1, sl 2 sts tog kwise, k1, p2sso, k1, [yo, k2tog] 2 times) 4 times—11 sts each section.

Rnd 19: ([SSK, yo] 2 times, sl 2 sts

tog kwise, k1, p2sso, [yo, k2tog] 2 times) 4 times—9 sts each section.

Rnd 21: (SSK, yo, k1, sl 2 sts tog kwise, k1, p2sso, k1, yo, k2tog) 4 times—7 sts each section.

Rnd 23: [SSK, yo, sl 2 sts tog kwise, k1, p2sso, yo, k2tog] 4 times—5 sts each section.

Rnd 25: [K1, sl 2 sts tog kwise, k1, p2sso, k1] 4 times—3 sts each section.

Rnd 27: [Sl 2 sts tog kwise, k1, p2sso] 4 times—1 st each section.

Cut thread, thread on to tapestry needle and run through rem sts, pull tight, and finish off. Weave in lose ends. Block.

New Palm Leaf Edging Doily

A purchased hemstitched doily edged with New Palm Leaf Edging is shown on page 86. The edging is attached to the doily as it is worked and then the beginning stitches are grafted to the ending stitches.

Thread: Size 10 crochet cotton: 1 ball (MC).
Needles: Size 1 (2.25 mm).
Notions: 9½" (24 cm) linen doily

round with hemstitching; waste thread in contrasting color; size 6 (1.8 mm) steel crochet hook; tapestry needle.

Preparation: Work 1 sc into every other hole of hemstitching. Join to first sc with a slip st. Finish off. Set aside.

Lace: With waste thread, CO 11 sts. Knit 4 rows. Change to MC.

Knit to last st, sl 1, k1 into sc in hemstitching, psso.

Note: After turning, slip all sts pwise with thread in front.

Row 1: Sl 1, k2, yo, k2tog, yo twice, k2tog, k2, yo twice, p2tog—13 sts.

Row 2: YO, p2tog, k5, p1, k4, sl 1, k1 into next sc, psso.

Row 3: Sl 1, k3, yo, k5, yo twice, k2tog, yo twice, p2tog—16 sts.

Row 4: YO, p2tog, k3, p1, k9, sl 1,

k1 into next sc, psso—16 sts.

Row 5: Sl 1, k4, yo, k3, yo twice, k2tog, k4, yo twice, p2tog—19 sts.

Row 6: YO, p2tog, k7, p1, k8, sl 1, k1 into next sc, psso.

Row 7: Sl 1, k5, yo, k9, k2tog, yo, p2tog.

Row 8: YO, p2tog, k16, sl 1, k1 into next sc, psso.

Row 9: Sl 1, k6, yo, k2tog, k6, k2tog, yo, p2tog—18 sts.

Row 10: YO, p2tog, k15, sl 1, k1 into next sc, psso.

Row 11: Sl 1, k7, yo, k2tog, k4, k2tog, yo, p2tog—17 sts.

Row 12: YO, p2tog, k14, sl 1, k1 into next sc, psso.

Row 13: Sl 1, k8, yo, [k2tog] 3 times, yo, p2tog—15 sts.

Row 14: YO, p2tog, k12, sl 1, k1 into next sc, psso.

Row 15: Sl 1, k7, k2tog, yo, k3tog, p2tog—12 sts.

Row 16: YO, p2tog, k2tog, k7, sl 1, k1 into next sc, psso—11 sts.

Rep Rows 1–16, attaching knitted edging to sc around doily as you go, ending with Row 16. (Skip 1 sc or work 2 sc in the same space if necessary to make knitted edging fit the number of sc's on the doily.) Do not BO. Remove waste thread and place live sts on needle. Cut thread, and use it to graft beg sts to end sts. Weave in loose ends. Block.

Table Runner

Delicate knitted lace finishes the ends of a woven table runner. The ends of the fabric are hemmed and the lace is sewn in place with sewing thread.

Thread: Normandy Linen Thread, 20/2 bleached white or Euroflax linen in desired color: 1 oz.

Needles: Size 2 (2.75 mm).

Notions: Linen fabric for embroidery or cross stitch with finished edges; matching sewing thread; sewing needle.

Edging: CO 20 sts. Knit 1 row. Work Rows 1–8 of Ladies' Home Journal Edging #2 (see page 39) 10 times, or until piece measures the width of the fabric slightly stretched. BO after Row 8.

Finishing: Block lace to fit edge of fabric. Make a 1/4" (6 mm) hem on the WS and tack in place with sewing thread. Place border over the hem and sew to the WS so that the edge of the lace completely covers the hem.

Diamond Edge Lace Mohair Scarf and Centerpiece

Yarn: *Scarf:* Prism Kid Mohair (125 yd [114 m]/oz): 4 oz; *Centerpiece:* Coats Patons Opera crochet cotton, size 10: 1 ball.

Needles: *Scarf:* Size 9 (5.5 mm); *Centerpiece:* Size 3 (3.25 mm).

Notions: Markers; stitch holder; tapestry needle.

- - - - - - - - - - - - - - -

Scarf

*CO 12 sts. Knit 1 row. Work Rows 1–12 of Diamond Edge Lace (see page 33) 3 times, then work Rows 1–6 again—15 sts.

Row 7: Sl 1, k1, psso, yo, k2tog, k1, yo, k2tog, yo, k8—15 sts.

Rows 8 and 10: Knit.

Row 9: Sl 1, k1, psso, k1, [yo, k2tog] 2 times, yo, k8—15 sts.

Row 11: Sl 1, k1, psso, k1, [yo, k2tog] 2 times, yo, k8—15 sts.

Row 12: BO 6 sts, k8—9 sts.

Row 13: Sl 1, k1, psso, k7—8 sts.

Rows 14 and 16: Knit.

Row 15: Sl 1, k7.

Rows 17, 19, 21 and 23: Rep Row 15.

Rows 18, 20, and 22: Rep Row 16.

Row 24: BO* but do not finish off. Leave rem st on needle, pick up and knit 43 sts along straighter edge of border—44 sts. *Next row:* K12, place marker, k20, place marker, k12. *Note:* slip markers every row.

Row 1: K8, yo, k2tog, yo, k2, k2tog, yo, k16, yo, k2tog, k2, yo, k2tog, yo, k8—46 sts.

Rows 2, 4, 6, 8, and 10: Knit.

Row 3: K8, yo, k1, k2tog, yo, k2, k2tog, yo, k16, yo, k2tog, k2, yo, k2tog, k1, yo, k8—48 sts.

Row 5: K8, [yo, k2tog] 2 times, yo, k2, k2tog, yo, k16, yo, k2tog, k2, [yo, k2tog] 2 times, yo, k8—50 sts.

Row 7: K8, yo, k2tog, yo, k1, k2tog, yo, k2, k2tog, yo, k16, yo, k2tog, k2, yo, k2tog, k1, yo, k2tog, yo, k8—52 sts.

Row 9: K8, [yo, k2tog] 3 times, yo, k2, k2tog, yo, k16, yo, k2tog, k2, [yo, k2tog] 3 times, yo, k8—54 sts.

Row 11: K8, [yo, k2tog] 2 times, yo, k1, k2tog, yo, k2, k2tog, yo, k16, yo, k2tog, k2, yo, k2tog, k1, [yo, k2tog] 2 times, yo, k8—56 sts.

Row 12: BO 6 sts, knit to end—50 sts.

Row 13: BO 6 sts, k7, yo, k2tog, yo, k2, k2tog, yo, k16, yo, k2tog, k2, yo, k2tog, yo, k8—46 sts.

Rep Rows 2–13 eighteen more times or to desired length. Then work Rows 2–12. *Next row:* BO 6, k7, turn—8 sts. Knit these 8 sts for 11 rows. BO these 8 sts. Place center 28 sts on holder. Knit rem 8 sts for 11 rows. BO these 8 sts. Finish off. Set aside.

Repeat border pattern from * to *. Finish off. Fit border between garter-st sections at both ends and center stitches. Graft edges together. Weave in loose ends. Do not block.

- - - - - - - - - - - - - - -

Centerpiece

CO 12 sts. Knit 1 row. Work Rows 1–12 of scarf 9 times or to desired length, working k20 instead of "k2tog, yo, k16, yo, k2tog". Finish as for scarf. Block.

These examples show how Diamond Edge Lace can be used for different effects. The scarf is worked with mohair, the centerpiece with crochet cotton. Each piece is begun by working the lace edging the length of one short end. Then stitches are picked up along the straight edge of the edging, and the body of the piece, including lace edging, is worked to the desired length.

Christening Dress

A ready-made christening dress and hat can become a family heirloom by adding knitted lace. The lower edging of the dress is Mrs. R's Diamond Lace (see page 41). The collar, cuffs, and hat trim are Imitation Torchon Lace (see page 33). Use the laces and number of repeats specified here as guidelines; what will work best for you depends on the size and style of christening dress and hat you use.

Thread: Coats Paton's Opera, Size 20: 2 balls. (Amount required will depend on the size of the dress.)

Needles: Size 1 (2.25 mm).

Notions: Plain christening dress, purchased or made from commercial pattern; sewing needle.

Lower edging: CO 27 sts. Knit 1 row. Work Rows 1–28 of Mrs. R's Diamond Lace (see page 41) until edging fits around hem of dress when slightly stretched. BO on Row 28.

Collar: (make 2) CO 11 sts. Knit 1 row. Work Rows 1–20 of Imitation Torchon Lace (see page 33) 4 times, or until collar fits around half of neck edge. BO on Row 20.

Cuffs: Work 5 repeats of Imitation Torchon Lace, or until piece fits around edge of sleeve.

Hat: Work 10 repeats of Imitation Torchon Lace, or until border fits over brim of hat.

Finishing: Block all borders to measurement of edge they are to be attached to. Sew the bottom border to the top of the dress hem. Press lightly to form pleats if desired. Fit the cuffs to the bottom of the sleeves. Attach the collars leaving the back neck and front neck open. Attach the border to the hat, fitting around the brim.

Heart Doily

Heart Lace forms a delicate edging on a hemstitched doily. A foundation of single crochet is worked into the hemstitching and then the lace edging is attached to the crochet as it is knitted. The beginning and ending edges are grafted together to make the design continuous around the doily.

Thread: Size 20 crochet cotton (MC): 1 ball.

Needles: Size 00 (1.75 mm).

Notions: 7" (18 cm) linen doily round with hemstitching; waste thread in contrasting color; size 8 (1.5 mm) steel crochet hook; tapestry needle.

Preparation: Work 1 sc into every hole of hemstitching. Join to first sc with a slip st. Do not finish off. Set aside.

Edging: With waste thread, CO 14 sts. Knit 4 rows. Slip last st from crochet edge onto right needle. Change to MC and knit across waste thread sts on left needle—15 sts. Knit to last st, sl 1, k1 into next sc, psso.

Note: After turning, slip all sts pwise with thread in front.

Row 1: Sl 1, k8, p1, yo, k1, yo, p1, k3—17 sts.

Row 2: K4, p3, k3, yo twice, k2tog, k4, sl 1, k1 into next sc, psso—18 sts.

Row 3: Sl 1, k6, p1, k2, p1, k1, [yo, k1] 2 times, p1, k3—20 sts.

Row 4: K4, p5, k10, sl 1, k1 into next sc, psso.

Row 5: Sl 1, k9, p1, k2, yo, k1, yo, k2, p1, k3—22 sts.

Row 6: K4, p7, k3, [yo twice, k2tog] 2 times, k3, sl 1, k1 into next sc, psso—24 sts.

Row 7: Sl 1, k5, [p1, k2] 2 times, p1, k7, p1, k3.

Row 8: K4, p7, k12, sl 1, k1 into next sc, psso.

Row 9: Sl 1, k11, p1, ssk, k3, k2tog, p1, k3—22 sts.

Row 10: K4, p5, k3, [yo twice, k2tog] 3 times, k3, sl 1, k1 into next sc, psso—25 sts.

Row 11: Sl 1, k5, [p1, k2] 3 times, p1, ssk, k1, k2tog, p1, k3—23 sts.

Row 12: K4, p3, k15, sl 1, k1 into next sc, psso.

Row 13: Sl 1, k14, p1, sl 1, k2tog, psso, p1, k3—21 sts.

Row 14: K20, sl 1, k1 into next sc, psso.

Row 15: Sl 1, k20.

Row 16: BO 6, k13, sl 1, k1 into next sc, psso—15 sts.

Rep Rows 1–16, attaching knitted edging to sc around doily as you go, ending with Row 16. (Skip 1 sc or work 2 sc in the same space if necessary to make knitted edging fit the number of sc's on the doily.) Do not BO. Remove waste thread and place live sts on needle. Cut thread and use it to graft beg sts to end sts. Weave in loose ends. Block.

Rose Point Doily

Rose Point Lace forms a delicate edging on a hemstitched doily. A foundation of single crochet is worked into the hemstitching and then the lace edging is attached to the crochet as it is knitted. The beginning and ending edges are grafted together to make the design continuous around the doily.

Thread: Size 30 crochet cotton (MC): 1 ball.

Needles: Size 000 (1.5 mm).

Notions: 9½" (24 cm) linen doily round with hemstitching; waste thread in contrasting color; size 9 (1.4 mm) steel crochet hook; tapestry needle.

Preparation: Work 1 sc into every hole of hem stitching. Join to first sc with a slip st. Do not finish off. Set aside.

Edging: With waste thread, CO 14 sts. Knit 4 rows. Slip last st from crochet edge onto right needle. Change to MC and knit across waste thread sts on left needle—15 sts. *Next row:* Knit to last st, work sl 1, k1, psso with st of sc to join to doily. *Note:* After turning, slip all sts pwise with thread in front.

Row 1: Sl 1, k2, yo, k2tog, k7, yo, k3—16 sts.

Row 2: K15, sl 1, k1 into next sc, psso.

Row 3: Sl 1, k2, yo, k2tog, k8, yo,

k3—17 sts.

Row 4: K16, sl 1, k1 into next sc, psso.

Row 5: Sl 1, k2, yo, k2tog, k9, yo, k3—18 sts.

Row 6: K17, sl 1, k1 into next sc, psso.

Row 7: Sl 1, k2, yo, k2tog, k3, k2tog, yo twice, k2tog, k3, yo, k3—19 sts.

Row 8: K9, p1, k8, sl 1, k1 into next sc, psso.

Row 9: Sl 1, k2, yo, k2tog, k1, k2tog, yo twice, k2tog twice, yo twice, k2tog, k2, yo, k3—20 sts.

Row 10: K8, p1, k3, p1, k6, sl 1, k1 into next sc, psso.

Row 11: Sl 1, k2, yo, k2tog, k3, k2tog, yo twice, k2tog, k5, yo, k3—21 sts.

Row 12: K11, p1, k8, sl 1, k1 into next sc, psso.

Row 13: Sl 1, k2, yo, k2tog, k1, k2tog, yo twice, k2tog twice, yo twice, k2tog, k3, yo, k2tog, k2.

Row 14: K4, k2tog, [k3, p1] 2 times, k6, sl 1, k1 into next sc, psso—20 sts.

Row 15: Sl 1, k2, yo, k2tog, k3, k2tog, yo twice, k2tog, k4, yo, k2tog, k2.

Row 16: K4, k2tog, k4, p1, k8, sl 1, k1 into next sc, psso—19 sts.

Row 17: Sl 1, k2, yo, k2tog, k10, yo, k2tog, k2.

Row 18: K4, k2tog, k12, sl 1, k1

into next sc, psso—18 sts.

Row 19: Sl 1, k2, yo, k2tog, k9, yo, k2tog, k2.

Row 20: K4, k2tog, k11, sl 1, k1 into next sc, psso—17 sts.

Row 21: Sl 1, k2, yo, k2tog, k8, yo, k2tog, k2.

Row 22: K4, k2tog, k10, sl 1, k1 into next sc, psso—16 sts.

Row 23: Sl 1, k2, yo, k2tog, k7, yo, k2tog, k2.

Row 24: K4, k2tog, k9, sl 1, k1 into next sc, psso.

Rep Rows 1–24, attaching knitted edging to sc around doily as you go, ending with Row 24. (Skip 1 sc or work 2 sc in the same space if necessary to make knitted edging fit the number of sc's on the doily.) Do not BO. Remove waste thread and place live sts on needle. Cut thread and use it to graft beg sts to end sts. Weave in loose ends. Block.

Delineator Leaf Lace Centerpiece

A piece of linen fabric is cut to the desired shape and the edges are serged. A row of slip-stitch crochet worked close to the surging provides the foundation for the Delineator Leaf Lace edging (see page 57), which is attached to the crochet as it is knitted. The beginning edge is grafted to the ending edge.

Thread: Size 10 crochet thread (MC): 1 ball.

Needles: Size 1 (2.25 mm).

Notions: Linen fabric cut to desired size (sample measures 14" by 9" [35.5 cm by 23 cm]); waste thread in contrasting color; size 7 (1.65 mm) steel crochet hook; tapestry needle.

Preparation: Serge or zigzag edges of fabric. With MC, work 1 row slip st inside the finished edge. Finish off.

Note: On straight edges of fabric, skip 2 sc for every 8 rows of pattern. For curved edges, skip 1 sc for every 8 rows of pattern. Border will be slightly puckered until blocked. Or, if preferred, knit the border and sew it to the rows of slip st in the fabric.

Edging: With waste thread, CO 25 sts. Knit 4 rows. Change to MC. Knit to last st, sl 1, k1, psso with last st and sc in hemstitching along the centerpiece.

Rows 1, 3, 5, and 7: Sl 1 with yarn in front, purl to end.

Row 2: [YO, k1, yo, k2, k2tog twice, k2] 2 times, [yo, k2tog] 3 times, sl 1, k1, psso with last st and next sc—25 sts.

Row 4: [YO, k3, yo, k1, k2tog twice, k1] 2 times, [yo, k2tog] 3 times, sl 1, k1, psso with last st and next sc.

Row 6: [YO, k5, yo, k2tog twice] 2 times, [yo, k2tog] 3 times, sl 1, k1, psso with last st and next sc.

Row 8: YO, k3, k2tog, k2, yo, k2tog, yo, k3, k2tog, k2, [yo, k2tog] 4 times, sl 1, k1, psso with last st and next sc.

Rep Rows 1–8, attaching knitted edging to sc around fabric as you go, ending with Row 7. (Skip 1 sc or work 2 sc in the same space if necessary to make knitted edging fit the number of sc's on the fabric.) Do not BO. Remove waste thread and place live sts on needle. Cut thread and use it to graft beg sts to end sts. Weave in loose ends. Block.

RESOURCES

Bibliography

Hiatt, June Hemmons. *The Principles of Knitting.* New York: Simon and Schuster, 1988.

Eaton, Jan. *A Creative Guide to Knitted Lace.* London: New Holland Limited, 1994.

Hewitt, Furze and Billie Daley. *Classic Knitted Cotton Edgings.* Kenthurst, New South Wales: Kangaroo Press, 1987.

Lace Knitting Supplies

Crochet/Knitting Threads, Crochet hooks
Coats Patons
1001 Roselawn Ave.
Toronto, Ontario, Canada M6B 1B8
(800)268-3620
www.coatspatons.com

DMC Company
South Hackensack Ave.
Port Kearny Bldg 10A
South Kearny, New Jersey 07032
(973)589-0606
www.dmc–usa.com

Mohair
Prism Yarns
2595 30th Ave N.
St Petersburg, Florida 33713
(813)327-3100

Cashmere
Hunt Valley Cashmere
6747 White Stone Road
Baltimore, Maryland 21207-4173
(410)298-8244

Cotton for Baby Sweater
Tahki
11 Graphic Place
Moonachie, New Jersey 07074
(201)807-0070

Lace needles, linen doily rounds, handkerchiefs, and various threads; acid free tissue paper and storage boxes
Lacis
3163 Adeline St.
Berkeley, California 94703
(510)843-7178
www.lacis.com

Linen thread, lace needle gauge, lace needles, linen doily rounds, and linen towels
Moonrise
2804 Fretz Valley Road
Perkasie, Pennsylvania 18944
(215)795-0345

Knitting needles and threads
Patternworks
Box 1690
Poughkeepsie, New York 12601
(800)438-5464
www.patternworks.com

Skacel
PO box 8810
Seattle, Washington 98138
(800)255-1278
www.skacelknitting.com

Nancie Knits
3214 Riverside Blvd.
Sacramento, California 95818
(800)867-2074

Blocking wires
Fiber Fantasy
6 Hunters Horn Court
Owings Mills, Maryland 21117
(800242-5648
www.fiberfan.com

INDEX